ACROSS THE SNOW MOUNTAINS

ACROSS THE SNOW MOUNTAINS

FROM TIBET TO EXILE

REBECCA S. ORTON

Across the Snow Mountains: From Tibet to Exile

Copyright © 2015 by Rebecca S. Orton.

All rights reserved. Printed and published in 2025 by White Tara Publishing, Washington USA.

No portion of this book may be reproduced in any form without written permission, except in the case of brief quotations embodied in critical articles and reviews with credit to the author or original source.

The author has used their best efforts in accurately preparing this book and makes no representations or warranties with respect to the accuracy or completeness of the contents. All opinions expressed are the author's.

FIRST EDITION

Hardback ISBN: 9798999760807

Paperback ISBN: 9798999760821

eBook ISBN: 9798999760814

Library of Congress Control Number (LCCN): 2025916939

Cover Photograph © Aniel Prudek (istock) reference 513247652

Map Illustrations: Julie Hale

Book design by Megan Sheer (sheerbookdesign.com)

For the Tsampa eaters

White Crane!
Lend me your wings.
I will not fly far.
From Lithang, I shall return.

Songs of the 6th Dalai Lama, Tsangyang Gyatso

CONTENTS

	Maps	ix
	Glossary	xi
	Introduction	1
Chapter 1	Bullets in the Snow	15
Chapter 2	On the Run	45
Chapter 3	Sisters	67
Chapter 4	The Long Pilgrimage	91
Chapter 5	China in Tibet	113
Chapter 6	Life in Exile	121
	Conclusion	131
	Notes	137
	Acknowledgemenrs	143
	Recommended Reading	147
	About the Author	149

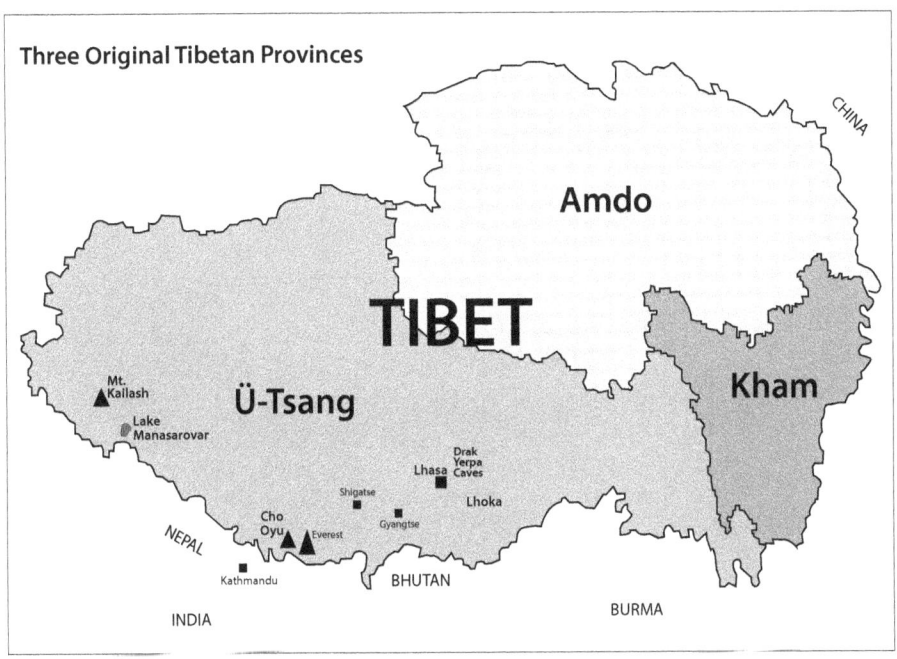

Map of Tibet showing the original territory, prior to China's invasion in 1950 and subsequent occupation, and points of interest visited by the women in this book on their journeys to India. When Tibetans speak of Tibet, this is the territory they are referring to.

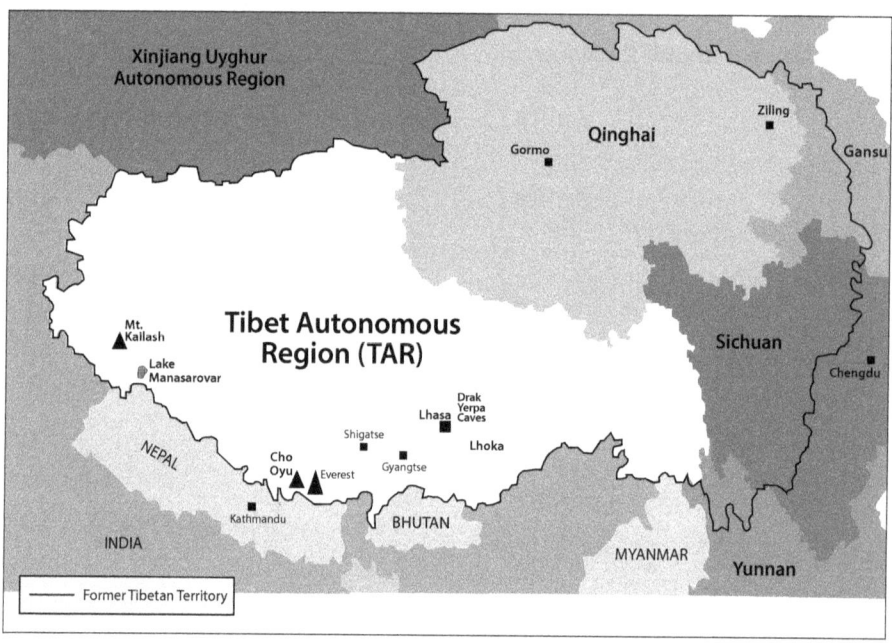

China has renamed the former Tibetan territories of Ü-Tsang, Amdo, and Kham, absorbed them into China, and created the Tibet Autonomous Region (TAR). The black line shows the former Tibetan territory.

GLOSSARY

chowk Hindi word referring to a marketplace, roundabout, or road junction. In McLeodganj, the main chowk consists mostly of a road junction with shops on all sides

churi dried cheese

kora circumambulation around a sacred site, a type of meditative practice common among Tibetans and Tibetan Buddhist practitioners. Many believe this practice brings merit to one's life

dri female yak

Gaden Phodrang Trust trust founded by the Fourteenth Dalai Lama to manage and support the institution of the Dalai Lama and its associated religious, cultural, and humanitarian activities. The organization is also entrusted with identifying and recognizing the next Dalai Lama

gen-la	teacher, pronounced with a hard "G." The addition of "-la" connotes respect
geshe, geshema	monk, nun. The equivalent of a PhD in Tibetan Buddhism
hungry ghosts	tortured souls caught in the cycle of rebirth in Tibetan Buddhist tradition. Many Tibetans who have grown up on the plateau speak convincingly of seeing ghosts near their homes or while out walking at night
inji	English-speaking person. Commonly used to refer to Westerners
khata	ceremonial silk scarf typically used in Tibetan and Mongolian cultures to denote respect, good will and auspiciousness. Most khatas are white and are offered to Buddhist teachers as a sign of respect. Often given at birthdays and weddings or to see travelers off on a journey, or draped over thangka scroll paintings
mala	Buddhist prayer string consisting of 108 beads, similar to a Catholic rosary or Islamic tasbih
mo dice	a form of divination, Tibetan mo dice are consulted when making decisions of great importance
Mönlam	the Aspiration Path. Every January, Tibetans gather at holy places to recite these prayers, with the intention that all beings attain enlightenment. Also known as the Great Prayer Festival, each sect of Tibetan Buddhism participates in Mönlam

Glossary

om mani padme hung (ཨོཾ་མ་ཎི་པདྨེ་ཧཱུྃ) — a mantra ubiquitous in Tibetan Buddhism, recited repeatedly and seen nearly everywhere: on rocks, flags, and in and around prayer wheels. There are somewhat varied translations of its meaning across the various sects of Buddhism, but it is most often expressed as "hail or praise to the jewel in the lotus," symbolizing compassion and spiritual growth for all beings

prostration — an act of humility, devotion, or submission, the entire length of the body is lain face down in front of Buddhist statues or respected Lamas. In this scenario, the prostration is performed three times. In some cases, prostration is repeated hundreds of times in an act of mental purification and devotion to the faith

Rinpoche — Tibetan word translated as "precious one" or "precious jewel." An honorific title, a Rinpoche is a highly realized teacher and/or a reincarnated tulku (Buddhist master)

sky burial — typical in many parts of Tibet, sky burial is a type of excarnation in which the body of the deceased is brought to a mountain top and fed to carrion and other wild animals. Born out of necessity in many parts of Tibet, where elevation above the tree line precludes cremation using firewood, and frozen ground prevents burial. Sky burial is also a lesson on impermanence and an act that brings merit for the deceased and their family, who are providing food for other living beings. The elaborate and lengthy ritual is usually carried out by a rogyapa (bone-breaker) or a monk. Typically, only high Lamas are cremated

snakehead	guide who escorts people out of Tibet. The term reflects their position at the head of a long line of people
stupa	with roots in pre-Buddhist burial mounds, stupas have become symbolic of the Buddha and his teachings and are sacred structures for prayer and meditation. They often contain relics of past spiritual masters
thangka	traditional Buddhist painting or appliqué on cotton and mounted on cloth framed by silk, with a silk drape over the front to protect the artwork when not being displayed. Thangkas depict Buddhist deities, mandalas, or religious scenes, and can be rolled up when not in use
Tibetan Transit School	Sherab Gotsel Lobling, also known as the Tibetan Transit School, was established in 1993 to provide education for newly arrived refugees between the ages of eighteen and thirty. The school provides English- and Tibetan-language instruction, computer and vocational courses, and dormitory quarters for students. The school provides the first ever formal education opportunity for many adult Tibetan students
tsampa	staple food of Tibet, consisting of roasted and ground barley, mixed by hand with butter tea, salt, dried cheese, and sometimes sugar, making a thick paste that is rolled into a ball and eaten. In recent years, Tibetans have labeled themselves as 'tsampa eaters' as a political statement to signify unity among all Tibetans, their shared cultural heritage, and connection to the land of Tibet, and opposition to Chinese rule

Tsuglagkhang Temple	sometimes referred to as the Dalai Lama's temple, located in McLeodganj, India
yartsa gunbu	a caterpillar fungus, *Ophiocordyceps sinensis*. Each spring, Tibetans scour the hillsides in search of the telltale spike attached to the caterpillar's head, which sticks up from the ground. Believed to be a health aid in China, it has become a multi-billion-dollar market

INTRODUCTION

For centuries, Tibetans have crossed the Himalayan Mountains on trading expeditions, on pilgrimages to India—the birthplace of Buddhism—and on diplomatic missions with their closest neighbors: Nepal, Bhutan, and India. Traditionally, Tibetans undertook the passage with horses, yaks, and plenty of supplies to ensure survival in the tempestuous climate of the world's highest mountains. Since China's invasion and occupation of Tibet in the 1950s, the nature of crossing the Himalayan Mountains has changed dramatically. With the Tibetan way of life upended by the Communists and amid destruction, repression, and forced acceptance of ideals that were antithetical to the Tibetan Buddhist way of life, Tibetans began to escape their homeland through the Himalayas without the benefit of pack animals or many weeks' worth of food.

The four stories captured in this book are examples of what escape through the Himalayas entails. There are many horror stories about the trek out of Tibet, most of them untold. Physical hardships—frostbite, starvation, snow blindness, and exhaustion—as well as stories of rape, abuse, capture, imprisonment, and torture are part of the standard narrative. While some published stories involve political prisoners or famous men like the Dalai Lama, the stories captured here are from women from simple backgrounds. Their journeys, which occurred between the early 1990s and early 2000s, represent some of the more common themes of the arduous trek across the Himalayas, though each journey is as unique as the woman who lived it.

How Tibetans manage to survive—if they do—and what happens to them along the way piqued my curiosity seventeen years ago when I first went to live in McLeodganj, in the upper portion of Dharamsala, India. I had volunteered for five months for one of the many NGOs in operation there, teaching English to exiled Tibetan adults. During that time, my students morphed into friends and confidants. When asked about how they had managed to get to India, they shared brief, standardized versions of their arduous treks from Tibet to India. The general narrative ran along the lines of, "It was very difficult, we ran out of food, it was cold, and I thought I was going to die." These truncated descriptions of what I imagined to be horrific journeys of epic proportions were merely an easy way to avoid a difficult topic. Four years later, unable to shake off my curiosity and belief that these were stories worth telling, I returned for an additional five months to conduct interviews for this book.

For those new to the subject of Tibet, it's helpful to begin with some historical context. This introduction provides a brief overview of some key events that prompted Tibetans to escape Tibet, and to continue doing so for decades. Further details regarding Tibet's modern history are threaded throughout the book, providing additional context about the issues facing Tibetans both inside Tibet and in exile. Most of the issues Tibetans face today are rooted in China's invasion of Tibet in 1950 and its subsequent occupation of the nation. The relationship between the Chinese Communist Party (CCP) and the Tibetan people reached a critical point in March 1959, when Tibetans revolted against the Chinese occupying their homeland, and His Holiness the Fourteenth Dalai Lama fled Lhasa, the capital city of Tibet, to the safety of India.

In 1950, one year after the CCP had gained control of China, the People's Liberation Army (PLA) invaded the eastern portion of the Tibetan nation. Under the auspices of freeing Tibet from "Imperialist" influence, the CCP set about bringing the rooftop of the world into the fold of the Motherland. From China's perspective, the Imperialists were Great Britain—former colonizer of India—and in small part the USA.

Tibetans did not welcome the Chinese, nor were they particularly concerned with Imperialist influences. In the years that followed, the Tibetan government in Lhasa tried to get along peaceably with the Chinese. But the ideological differences between the Tibetan Buddhist way of life and Communist ideals were at such great odds that by 1959, the barely tenable relations had unraveled entirely. In late winter 1959, Tibetans from the eastern provinces began gathering in Lhasa, for the days-long Mönlam prayer festival. With them they brought tales of brutality against monks and nuns, torture, imprisonment, and murder, all at the hands of the PLA. These violent actions against the Tibetan people contradicted the autonomy, religious freedom, and slow rollout of Communist reforms that Chairman Mao had promised the young Fourteenth Dalai Lama five years prior. Tibetans were unhappy, and tensions in Lhasa were mounting.

While thousands of Tibetans were gathered in the city for Mönlam, a rumor spread that the Chinese planned to abduct the Dalai Lama from Norbulingka, his summer palace. The fear that their beloved leader was in danger further ignited their anger, discontent, and desperation, and in short order, Tibetans gathered outside the gates of the palace to protect him. Day and night, thousands camped outside the palace gates, not allowing anyone to enter. Protests moved through Lhasa's streets with signs saying, "Tibet is for Tibetans," a common rallying slogan that conveyed that China was not welcome. The PLA responded with arrests and gunfire, later executing those who had led the protests. Behind the palace walls, the twenty-three-year-old Dalai Lama, the nation's spiritual leader and head of the Tibetan government, faced an impossible decision. His family and advisors urged him to flee the city; Tibet's future counted on his survival, thus his safety must be protected at all costs. Yet the last thing he wanted to do was abandon his people. Over the next several days, he searched inwardly and outwardly for an answer. Consulting oracles and advisors, he remained steadfast that he would not abandon his country.

Finally, after the PLA shelled the Norbulingka, the Dalai Lama's advisors managed to convince him to leave the city and seek refuge in India. On March 17, 1959, dressed as a soldier, he and a small escort of trusted advisors also costumed as Tibetan soldiers were able to move past the throngs of angry Tibetans outside the palace gates.

Among those attending the prayer festival were men and women who had formed the Tibetan militia in the early 1950s, consisting mostly of people from the eastern provinces of Amdo and Kham. Anticipating a rebellion, and equipped only with antiquated rifles and artillery, these militia fighters had set up strongholds throughout Lhasa and in the hills overlooking the city. While the Dalai Lama wrestled with a choice he didn't want to make, the Tibetan militia was readying for battle. By the time the Norbulingka was shelled, the Tibetan revolt had already begun. The militia and an ever-increasing number of volunteers responded to the PLA as best they could; with antiquated arms and ingenuity, they fiercely defended their nation's freedom. Eventually, they were overrun by the modern Chinese army, and the rebellion was put down. By that time, the Dalai Lama was threading his way through the mountains on his way to India.

Occupied by the melee in the city, the Chinese were at first unaware that the Dalai Lama had escaped. But soon, Tibet's leader was in a race against time, as he made his way across the Himalayas with the Chinese close on his heels. With the entire world waiting for news of Tibet's "God-King" and his flight from the Communists, roughly two weeks after fleeing Lhasa, he arrived safe at the Indian border, free to denounce China's presence in his country.

Over the next few years, in the Dalai Lama's wake, an exodus of about 80,000 Tibetans left the country. During the following decades, Tibetans continued to escape their homeland—sometimes in large numbers during years of intense unrest. For a long period, between 2,500 and 3,000 Tibetans made their way annually through the Himalayas, seeking blessings from the Fourteenth Dalai Lama and refuge from China's repression. The journey is considered illegal, and punishable, by the People's Republic of China (PRC), which for seventy-five years has obstinately claimed that Tibet has always been part of China—a claim consistently refuted by Tibetans.

Early in China's occupation, Tibetans left Tibet due to the violence the PLA meted out against the population, as well as a number of atrocities that trampled upon their freedom. This included forced acceptance of Communist ideologies, the destruction of monasteries, mistreatment of monks and nuns, imprisonment, incarceration in forced labor camps, and the repression of religion and culture. The years of the Cultural Revolution and the failure of the Great Leap Forward brought unnecessary hardship to all who lived under Chinese rule. No one was spared, except for China's Communist leaders and those faithful to Chairman Mao.

Introduction

In the decades after the 1960s, the reasons for abandoning Tibet began to have fewer political underpinnings. That's not to say that religious persecution or political issues didn't exist in Tibet; they did, and still do, but statistically most Tibetans who left home for India in the 1990s through the early-2000s were bent on receiving the auspicious blessings of the Dalai Lama at least once in their lifetime. A pilgrimage to receive blessings from Tibet's spiritual and temporal leader is of monumental importance, fueled in part by mythical beliefs. The Dalai Lama is a real flesh-and-blood man whose stature, through his decades-long absence from the holy city of Lhasa, has grown to mythic proportions. He is revered as the soul of Tibet. In China-occupied Tibet, it is illegal to own a picture of the Dalai Lama, even speaking his name is punishable. Tenzin Gyatso—the Fourteenth Dalai Lama's absence from Tibet, has created an unquenchable longing among Tibetans residing there that has rendered him far more important than ever. By far, Tenzin Gyatso is the most famous of all the Dalai Lamas. His fame and numerous international accolades have secured his prominence in the minds and hearts of Tibetans, especially those in Tibet, many of whom fear dying before having seen him. And this is precisely why so many risk their lives to cross the Himalayas into Nepal and eventually make their way to McLeodganj. They long to see the living Buddha, Chenrezig, Avalokiteshvara—the Bodhisattva of Compassion, Kundun—the Presence, Amitabha—the eternal Buddha, the Fourteenth Dalai Lama—Ocean of Wisdom. Jetsun Jamphel Ngawang Lobsang Yeshe Tenzin Gyatso has many lofty and honorable names for a man who views himself as a simple Buddhist monk. The reality of the dangerous journey to India is usually not well considered, nor is the life that awaits them in India or Nepal, where they will find that they have become exiled, trapped in limbo.

While the Dalai Lama is the number-one reason Tibetans journey across the Snow Mountains (གངས་རི in Tibetan script, gang ri, "snow mountain"; a mountain with snow is simply referred to as a "Snow Mountain" unless the mountain has a specific name), education is a secondary motive for leaving home and hearth. Monks and nuns often seek Tibetan Rinpoches in Nepal and India, who are free of China's repressive interference, to guide them through the labyrinth of Tibetan Buddhist study. Parents send their young children across the mountains with relatives or trusted Lamas to attend Tibetan-run schools throughout India. And yes, there are those who leave for all the above reasons.

In recent decades, to reach India, Tibetans have walked across the Himalayas guided by *snakeheads*, men paid to see them safely through the mountains. Inadequately outfitted to survive the ferocious conditions, Tibetans undertake the trek without the benefit of below-zero sleeping bags, well-made hiking boots, winterized clothing, or large backpacks filled with survival gear and space-age food supplies, let alone horses and yaks, as in the past. Instead, they traverse the world's highest mountain range in sneakers or cheap boots, jeans, monks' and nuns' robes, basic winter jackets, or traditional Tibetan chubas made of yak or sheep wool, and barely enough food to last a week. Some carry small backpacks, sleeping bags, or woolen blankets and extra shoes and socks, but none are equipped to survive below-freezing temperatures and mountain passes as high as 19,000 feet for three or more weeks—and yet most of them do.

Once across the mountains, they have typically made their way to the Tibetan Refugee Transit Center (TRTC) in Kathmandu, Nepal. In conjunction with the United Nations High Commissioner for Refugees (UNHCR), the Tibetan Welfare Office processes each refugee. The TRTC provides food, clothing, shelter, and medical care. After being processed as refugees in Nepal, most eventually make their way to Dharamsala and the little hilltop town of McLeodganj, home to the Dalai Lama since 1959, as well as the well-organized Central Tibetan Administration (CTA), the exiled government of Tibet. There, they have an opportunity to meet with and receive blessings from their beloved leader.

The Indian government has generously supported Tibetan refugees by providing funds and land for settlements since the Dalai Lama's arrival in 1959. India now hosts forty-five Tibetan settlements throughout the country, with a current population of roughly 80,000—a decline from 150,000 in 2011. Settlements in Bhutan and Nepal also host Tibetan refugees. Though not the largest Tibetan settlement in India, Dharamsala—with its proximity to the Dalai Lama and the CTA, and McLeodganj, known as "Little Lhasa," a nod to Tibet's capital city—is the heart of the diaspora.

Introduction

Perched along a ridge high above the Kangra Valley, McLeodganj was once a hill station used by the British Raj to escape the summer heat of India's plains. Flanked by the southernmost edge of the Himalayas, the town boasts a ruggedly majestic view of the Dhauladhar Range's snow-covered peaks and a sweeping view of the Kangra Valley below. The town is a slice of exiled Tibet that at first glance appears enchanting: a charming replica of Tibetan culture in India. There are as many Tibetan businesses as Indian bordering the town's three narrow streets, each relying on foreign and, increasingly, domestic tourism to survive. The town lures tourists to the area, the main attractions being the Dalai Lama, his temple, and his exiled compatriots, as well as the mountains, winter snows, and the cooler temperatures of the high altitude. Pandering to those tourists, cafes and restaurants dish up everything from Tibetan momos and thentuk—a Tibetan noodle soup—to wood-fired pizza, brownies, cappuccinos, and, of course, Indian fare.

With the increasing number of Indian tourists flocking to the area year-round, the traffic along the narrow, twisting mountain road leading to McLeodganj is often bumper-to-bumper, choking to a crawl at the main chowk before turning onto Bhagsu Road, where many visitors head to hotels near the Bhagsunag Falls and a public swimming pool. Signaling the start of each day at five a.m., slow, rhythmic gongs from nearby monasteries ride the air currents, along with the fragrance of puja fires from Tibetans and Indians observing morning prayer rituals.

Overnight buses arriving from Delhi deposit road-weary travelers onto the streets of a barely waking town. Colorful Tibetan prayer flags flutter from buildings whose rooftops and balcony railings create a superhighway for rhesus macaque monkeys to roam and forage in the town, stealing food from homes whose owners have carelessly left windows or doors open. Packs of feral dogs soak up the sun along the roadsides, resting from a long night of barking and carousing, and cows meander through the streets as in many Indian cities, casually stealing vegetables from roadside stalls or from the bags of unsuspecting shoppers. By nine a.m., shopkeepers open well-worn metal doors to begin a ten-or twelve-hour workday, and the residents of the colorful but grimy buildings begin their morning ablutions as the small hilltop town comes to life.

Life among the exiles is complicated, camouflaged by the dominant narrative exemplified by His Holiness the Dalai Lama, who is often viewed by the West as the personification of all Tibetans. He's a wonderful human to have as a spiritual leader, but his persona should not be conflated with all Tibetans'. Though he has continuously denied enlightenment and describes himself as a simple monk who sometimes has a temper, His Holiness is revered the world over—except in China, where he is vilified as a splittist and a wolf in sheep's clothing. In the eyes of the West, Tibetan culture, its religion, its people, and the Dalai Lama are sacred and unique, and many have suggested that Tibetan culture holds the key to curing the disease of the Western world—namely, our unhappiness and self-centered materialism. There is a historical tendency to romanticize Tibetans in ways that objectify them. Tibetans are human, and thus as fallible as the rest of us. They don't hold special knowledge or secrets to solve the world's problems. Tibetans are merely people who have found themselves on the losing side of history.

The earliest Western visitors referred to Tibet as a hidden kingdom, lost to time. The Tibetan people and culture were in many ways confusing—poor but gracious hosts, resilient and spiritually devoted, with a sophisticated administrative and monastic education system, contrary to the living conditions of lay people, which were quite rustic. The early twentieth-century explorer and longtime resident of Tibet Alexandra David-Néel wrote, "Tibet is not a land, but a world … It is the kingdom of the spirit, where miracles are born of solitude." Thomas Manning, the first Englishman to reach Lhasa in 1811, noted, "Tibet is a country wrapped in silence. It is simple, poor, and strange—but there is a peace here I have never known elsewhere." Early visitors to Tibet were understandably amazed to discover what must have seemed a very strange land and people, who were intensely devoted to Buddhism and had over time developed an elaborate form of the religion. Many of the stereotypes about Tibetans that sprang from those early explorers continued into the twentieth century. The 1933 James Hilton novel *Lost Horizon* created the Shangri-La fiction, influencing the Western view of the "Roof of the World" as a utopia of peace and tranquility, further cementing the Tibetan myth in Western minds.

While it's true that in many ways Tibet was a land lost to time, largely pre-industrial with no forms of modern transportation—highways, airports, cars, and trains did not exist in the nation prior to China's invasion—Shangri-La it was not. However, Tibetans were devoted to the monastic system and study of Buddhism, believing that everyone was better off when surrounded by a culture of spiritual endeavor, and some who were able to visit Tibet prior to the 1950s were mystified by the impact their experience had on them spiritually.

My introduction to Tibet in the late 1980s included the same language used by early explorers. The religious, spiritual, and mystical tropes were intact then, and still are today, when Westerners speak of Tibetans with awe, suggesting that Tibetans are gentle, peaceful vegetarians who wouldn't dream of hurting a soul. To put them on a pedestal, to extol their virtues without a sense of reality, is to commit a great disservice to a people whose political plight is one of the most ignored, least understood, and most significant examples of global hegemony today. Idolizing Tibetans, whether the Dalai Lama or others, ignores the struggles of displacement and the trials of living a largely powerless life, estranged from home and family or dominated by an occupier bent on destroying Tibetan culture except where it is of use to China.

I carried many of these stereotypes with me on my first visit to India and McLeodganj. Thankfully, they were ripped away shortly after I arrived in the mountaintop town. The Hollywoodized versions of Tibetans I had come to accept as truth contradicted the drunken young men hitting on me in restaurants or following me through the streets, as did tales of knife fights, murder, opportunism, and archaic superstitions. On my first visit, I was shocked and disappointed that *these people* didn't live up to my expectations. The stereotypes I had accepted without question objectified and limited who Tibetans were allowed to be, while obscuring the more complex realities of the culture and their condition as exiles in India. Rather than allow my disappointment to color my perspective, I forged ahead with a sense of curiosity. During my first trip in particular, teaching and building relationships were an essential part of my learning. On both trips, I settled in as a temporary winter resident of McLeodganj.

When I returned to India for a second visit, specifically to conduct interviews for this book and to study the Tibetan language, much had changed—and yet much had not. The number of Indian tourists had skyrocketed, as had prices. More Tibetans were gainfully employed than on my previous visit, and those who had been raised in Tibet were more eager to return home than to go abroad; their longing for their rightful homeland was far more acute than I had experienced before.[1] But returning to Tibet is no easy feat, and if one is successful, the price paid is the loss of freedom and being subjected to intense scrutiny.

Left to my imagination, I often wondered what it would feel like to live in a country not my own, without citizenship, without a passport, without the freedom to return home or travel elsewhere at any time of my choosing. One Tibetan friend summed it up succinctly in an exchange she had with a European student she was tutoring in the Tibetan language. After telling her how lucky she was to live in such a beautiful place as McLeodganj, so near to His Holiness and with so much freedom to relax and enjoy life, she gave him an earful, saying, "If you think that is true, then give me your passport, your IDs, your birth certificate, all of your money, and any way you have to go home, and then let's see how wonderful it is for you."

The more time I spent with Tibetan exiles, the more I began to see the cracks in the armor of smiles and laughter that each of my students and close friends wore. For many, depression simmered just below the surface, brought on by deep homesickness and a perpetual state of powerlessness. Life as a refugee or an exile permanently displaced from home and family is not the goal Tibetans set out with when they leave Tibet. Nor is it something they imagine or anticipate. Once in India or Nepal, they find themselves stuck in a harsh reality, living a life with limited possibilities. Returning home is foremost in the minds of many, but it's a complicated undertaking. Understandably, few are willing to repeat in reverse the long, arduous journey across the mountains, and the odds of returning legally are slim—though both do occur. Thus, life is lived in a state of permanent limbo, facing a future with few—if any—familial ties and estrangement from a place whose importance, like the Dalai Lama, has grown to fairy-tale proportions.

Introduction

In the accounts that follow are stories of terror, murder, grief, adventure, regret, and even humor. With my friend Dechen as translator, I asked each participant if they were willing to share their stories to be published in a book; all of them agreed. I eventually focused on four women whose stories represented some of the more common themes, while also being extraordinary. We met in my room during the cold months of northern India's winter, with the space heater at our feet and plenty of hot water, tea, and blankets to keep us warm; housing in India is primarily of concrete and rebar, with no insulation or central heating—lovely in the hot summer months but quite cold in the high-altitude winter. Recording the interviews on my laptop, each woman related her experience in the Tibetan language, allowing her the freedom of expression. Dechen translated to English after each of my questions had been answered. As we talked back and forth in English and Tibetan, we also laughed and cried together. In the weeks prior to the interviews, I had become friends with each woman and heard bits of their stories, so I was confident that the opportunity to elaborate on what I already knew would provide a solid overview of life in Tibet, the journey across the mountains, and life in exile.

Even though none but Dechen spoke English with any proficiency, somehow, we managed to transcend language to forge friendships that last to this day. Each woman was kind enough to indulge my curiosity in the hope that others would learn of their lives. They generously answered questions that forced them to open old wounds and difficult memories. For that, I am grateful. Out of concern for the lives of each woman and her remaining family in Tibet, I have used aliases to protect their identities.

We begin with Lhamo's story. Introduced to me by a mutual friend, I was taken aback to discover she was part of the group whose trek became an international incident in 2006, when a nun was murdered, shot in the back while trying to flee across a high mountain pass. The Chinese border police's attack on Tibetans crossing the Nangpa La Pass marked the first time hard evidence corroborated what Tibetans had claimed for years: that crossing the mountains meant facing not only the perils of the Himalayas, but also those of human-perpetrated violence. Lhamo's story is a terrifying testament to the dangers of crossing the Snow Mountains and the persistent effects of trauma and China's determination to prevent Tibetans from leaving the occupied territory.

While shopping along the streets of McLeodganj one afternoon, I met a very friendly Tibetan man at his jewelry stall, who insisted on introducing me to his wife. Kunchok's English was very basic but far better than my Tibetan, and I understood he wanted me to follow him to their home. As we walked, he told me his wife was seven months pregnant. As we passed the main chowk, a petite, very pregnant woman appeared from the crowd. With one gold-plated incisor peeking out from her friendly smile, Dolma was brimming with chatter. She put her arm in mine and chatted animatedly in Tibetan while walking me to her home. Kunchok, in the moments he was around, attempted to translate what Dolma was saying, but most of the time I didn't have a clue; yet we became like sisters, bonding largely without language. Slowly I learned that life for Dolma had rarely been easy before or after she had reached India, and yet she exemplified the tenacity to survive regardless of the adversity that crossed her path. Forced by financial debt to the Chinese government, she took on the unimaginable, trekking with her two very young daughters across the world's most formidable mountains to escape the certainty of prison. And her story didn't end there.

Through another friend, I met the Tibetan nun Ani B, a most delightful and merry soul who became my study partner (ani is the Tibetan word for nun). Our goal was to teach each other our respective languages, and each afternoon we met for conversation. Our attempts were rarely successful and often led to confusion and laughter. As a devout nun, Ani B left her family out of devotion to the Buddhist faith. In India, she could study undeterred with some of the best and most sought-after Rinpoches and Lamas, such as the Seventeenth Karmapa, the head of the Kagyu lineage of Tibetan Buddhism. Determined to devote her life to Buddhism, she was committed fully to her faith, even when she had to leave behind the person she loved the most.

Last, Dechen. We met during my first visit to India and have maintained a friendship ever since. She was my trusted translator and agreed to tell me her story, which begins at the age of nine. Before making her way to India, she embarked on a two-year pilgrimage across the vast and mostly wild lands of Tibet with her mother. Her memories of that time remain alive in her adult mind, seemingly unblemished by her age or the more than twenty years she lived in India. She related the story from the perspective of the young child she was then, often laughing at her childish naïveté. As a nomad from the eastern portion of Tibet, she knew nothing of the world beyond the grazing lands and mountains in her domain. She was a young girl on an adventure with her mother, whom she viewed as her protector, a strong, invincible woman. Bits of Dechen's mother's life, having grown up during the Cultural Revolution and the Great Leap Forward, are included as historical background to Dechen's story. During their long pilgrimage, young Dechen was introduced to a modern world that sometimes terrified her in ways that she now finds uproariously humorous. Once an ignorant little girl sheltered by a nomadic life, through her travels, education, and experiences, Dechen is now an astute and articulate woman.

All but one of the women's lives have changed in positive and all-encompassing ways. Each touched my soul and heart as our friendships grew into a sort of sisterhood. On this visit, I wasn't gen-la or inji; I was acha-la (older sister) and tomo-la (friend), and I recognized the privilege granted me to gain entrance into what was for many a painful remembrance of a time better forgotten and of a place so close and yet so very far from their reach. It is with these women and many others in mind that I endeavor to capture and share their stories, and to them I dedicate this book.

CHAPTER 1

BULLETS IN THE SNOW

In the wide expanse of the Tibetan Plateau, there was no place to hide from the deep, resonant rumble and blinding claws streaking across the sky that would send Lhamo scampering under her mother's chuba for safety. As a little girl, she feared that the growling monsters, with their flashing daggers racing across the vast sky, would reach into the yak-wool tent and tear her apart. Many years later, when the thunder roared, she would increase the TV's volume and huddle deep into her pink winter jacket, safe inside her small room in the hills of Dharamsala, India. "Om mani padme hung, om mani padme hung"; reciting the prayer calmed her. In these moments she also remembered the foolish young girl she once had been, believing in monsters and gods crashing around in the sky. She knew now that thunder and lightning were just weather, not angry gods, though the sound still heightened her anxiety and made her feel a sense of panic. Lhamo had also learned that there were real monsters right here on earth, walking among us. Every crack of lightning sounded like gunfire ringing off the icy Himalayan slopes and sent her reeling back in time. Standing at the window, watching the rain fall and the flashes of light race across the night sky, Lhamo would remind herself that the terror of the 19,000-foot Nangpa La Pass was over, and that she was safe in McLeodganj, India.

Lhamo was a long way from her life as a nomad, and yet, life was hard in a way it hadn't been in Tibet. Replaced mostly by modern conveniences, activities like collecting and drying dung for the fire and hauling water from the river were a memory. Running water was just outside her door, along with a squat toilet. She used a propane burner for cooking, and in the winter a small electric space heater kept her warm. She had a cell phone and knew how to use a computer, something she had never imagined even existed in her previous life, following the animals across the vast Tibetan Plateau. She hadn't milked a goat or dri or churned cream into butter for a very long time. Except on special occasions, she wore jeans and sneakers instead of a chuba, and carried a purse to the market. Her skin had transformed from dark and ruddy to fair and faintly freckled. Her auburn, hennaed hair, smelling sweet from shampoo, and her glossy ponytail were vastly different from the multiple butter-greased braids she used to wear. Her beloved Tibet was nothing more than a precious memory.

Yet, she missed her homeland and her family and often dreamed of returning to Tibet. Seeing her parents once again was unlikely, but she continued to hope for a reunion. Above all, Lhamo was lonely. She disliked living alone and was happiest when relatives or friends crowded into her tiny room. Cooking up a large pot of thentuk or making momos while swapping stories, trading idle gossip, and laughing at silly jokes was one of her favorite activities. During these moments, her worries about her future dissipated, only to quickly return when her guests were gone. Would she always live alone, or might she someday marry and have children? Would she ever see the green hills of her former home, the endless blue sky, or her mother? Or was she stuck forever in India? These were the questions that invaded her mind day after day while working in the tailoring shop or upon waking in the early morning.

Looking back, Tibet seemed like a perfect idyll—a life she had rejected and could reach only through turning over the memories of past ghosts. India had become her home, and Lhamo was an exile. It was not exactly the life of her childish daydreams. During her sprouting adolescence, Lhamo had had a sense of wanting more. Something had pulled at her, drawing her away from the simple world she knew. During the summer festivals, she would sit with the adults at night and listen intently to their stories of faraway places, difficult times, and the beloved Kundun. While the adults talked about pilgrimages to Lhasa, sacred sites like Mt. Kailash, and the greatness of revered Lamas, she felt a stirring in her chest and imagined herself one day experiencing these places and people. Whether real or imagined, she had felt that whatever lay beyond the Snow Mountains beckoned her, even as she followed the grazing animals over the summer-greened hills of her home in eastern Tibet.

Unknowingly, her mother had fed Lhamo's fantasies when she had sometimes spoken reverently about the sacred Kundun. As she had smoothed and plaited her daughter's long, black hair, she had shared with Lhamo the same tales told to her by her own mother about life before the Fourteenth Dalai Lama had fled to India in 1959. When the Chinese had come, everything had changed. Their peaceful lives had been destroyed in so many ways, but the loss of Tibet's beloved leader to a faraway land was a pain none of the elders seemed able to move beyond. Her relatives had spoken of His Holiness in hushed tones, sometimes so overcome with emotion their voices would crack, their faces contorting to control the sadness. Crying in front of others only created more unhappiness; it was best to keep it contained.

Not long after Mao Zedong and the Chinese Communist Party (CCP) took control of China in 1949, Chinese soldiers began infiltrating the eastern part of Tibet, then known as Kham. It wasn't long before the fierce Khampas began to rebel. They hid in the mountains and fought against the Chinese People's Liberation Army (PLA). Many villagers died or were imprisoned for their rebellion. Some of Lhamo's relatives had been among the early resisters, whose efforts would continue for more than two decades. As the new People's Republic of China (PRC) sought control of the people and land of Tibet, fear, violence, and mostly unwelcome changes crept into the villages dotted across the nearly one million square miles of the remote Buddhist country.

After nine years of occupation and amid increasing turmoil, pressure to adopt Communist principles, and the threat of persecution, the Dalai Lama sought safety in India. There, he could freely broadcast his plea for help to the world and remain safe from possible retaliation from the CCP. Torn from his people in Tibet, he now lived in a beautiful temple in India—or so Lhamo's mother believed. A pilgrimage to see him just once in a person's lifetime would bring auspicious rewards and a sense of completion to a simple life. Lhamo's mother had never mustered the courage to undertake the long and dangerous journey to India, and, like her grandmother, she would die without ever seeing His Holiness in person. Lhamo didn't want to follow in her mother's footsteps—of that, she was certain.

By the time she turned twenty-one, Lhamo had grown restless and impatient, as if something inside her were clawing to the surface. Sitting on the hillsides, watching the yaks and dri graze, Lhamo would close her eyes and imagine the magical land called India. She saw herself receiving a blessing from *Kundun*—the living Buddha—and her heart instantly filled with joy. Many Tibetans were willing to risk their lives crossing the mountains just to bask in the presence of His Holiness for a few minutes. Since he is not allowed to return to Tibet, many risk everything to go to him. Lhamo wanted this too; however, the thought of her parents' certain disapproval of such a journey would abruptly end her fantasy and fill her with disappointment. She ached to go. If she left, she hoped that her father and mother would forgive her.

Growing up as a nomad in one of the most remote places on earth, Lhamo was uneducated; even in the twenty-first century, she had very little knowledge of or access to the world beyond Tibet. Her best friend Pema, her co-conspirator who shared Lhamo's fantasies, was no different. From the tales they heard from villagers and other nomads who had traveled to Lhasa and beyond, the girls spun inspired fantasies filled with adventure and promise. They marveled at the possibilities that awaited them beyond the endless plateau of home. In secret and despite their parents' certain disapproval, they began to construct a plan to leave their nomadic life.

"Pema-la, meet me by the river," Lhamo often whispered to her friend. At the designated meeting spot, they filled their buckets with water and sat on the bank talking until dark.

"We can go as soon as we have enough money."

"How much do we need?"

Neither girl really knew what it would take to get to Lhasa. Always considerate of their parents, Pema reminded Lhamo of their duties. "Lhamo-la, we must wait until the harvest is over."

"Yes, yes, we can't leave our families with so much work. But we can't wait long, or the weather will be too bad."

Long before they truly understood the journey they were undertaking, Lhamo and Pema decided to walk to the holy city of Lhasa from their village near Chamdo. They didn't know it was 700 miles; they only knew that other Tibetans walked to Lhasa on a regular basis. Going on long pilgrimages and walking great distances was a way of life. Occasionally, someone owned a motorcycle, but mostly one rode a horse or walked. They both thought of the journey not as a hardship, but as one piece of a larger goal.

Lhamo knew from the stories she heard that she would need a guide to help her cross the mountains to India. She and Pema would work in Lhasa and save money to hire one of the snakehead guides they'd heard talk of. Then they would meet with the Dalai Lama. Laid out in this step-by-step manner, their plan seemed neat and simple; the reality, however, was far more dangerous and complicated than either girl knew to imagine.

By late summer of 2004, the girls were ready to set out for Lhasa. With a bit of money and favorable late-summer weather, the time was right. Earlier in the day, Lhamo packed a small bag with some clothes, tsampa, cheese, and a water container, which she hid under yak pelts. Late that night, after taking one last look at her sleeping family, she crept from her home. There would be no tearful goodbyes or protests from her parents; Lhamo was running away from home not because she hated her parents, but because adventure and the Dalai Lama beckoned. The cool air filled her lungs as she quickly stepped outside and closed the tent flaps behind her. Glancing at the glittering web far above her head, her breath and the thud of her heartbeat were unnaturally loud when enveloped in the silence of this remote place. At the riverbank, Lhamo and Pema broke into uncontrollable giggles and animated conversation as they scurried farther away from the only way of life they had ever known.

Late summer was transforming the vivid emerald hues of spring to wheat-gold, and though the glacially fed rivers were lower than they had been only a few weeks previous, crossing them was still difficult—and there were many to cross. Up and over steep hills, Lhamo and Pema strolled unhurried until they met with a road. Catching a ride in one of the big trucks would speed their progress across the plateau, a tip they had learned from years of eavesdropping on adult conversations. They walked for an uneventful few days before finding a road and a truck driver who allowed them to ride in the back. The speed with which they were able to travel was not lost on either girl. The wind in their faces and sense of adventure diminished the bumpiness of the ride and felt like freedom. Entering the Lhasa Valley with an oxygen-deprived altitude of 12,000 feet and surrounded by snow-encrusted peaks, Lhamo and Pema began to realize they were close to achieving their goal. Happily enjoying the view from the bed of the truck, they chatted about what Lhasa would be like.

The ancient holy capital of Tibet, home to the Dalai Lama for nearly 500 years, was now modernized. Traffic cluttered the streets. Modern buildings were springing up all over the city, taking the place of the older structures that had reflected Tibet's unique architecture. Mandarin Chinese letters Lhamo could not read filled signs along roadways and above shop doors. Shockingly, brothels were in abundance, with scantily clad young girls selling their bodies from the doorways. Pema and Lhamo giggled with shock and embarrassment and hurried past the brothels; these were not images of their daydreams.

The bustling city was as exciting as it was confusing. Never had the girls seen so many people or heard such a cacophony. Nothing in their wildest imaginings could have prepared them for the chaos of the city and the impact of the magnificent Potala Palace. Hovering 384 feet high on Marpo Ri (Red Hill), the Potala is a commanding presence above the city. A splendid example of Tibetan architecture and sacred art, the rammed-earth-and-stone structure consists of the Red and White Palaces, protective walls, and a series of formidable broad staircases. It is thirteen stories at its highest and contains 698 murals, 1,000 rooms, and nearly 10,000 thangkas, as well as many precious objects of jade, gold, and silver. Construction of the historically significant white-and-red structure began modestly in the seventh century at the order of King Songsten Gampo. In the mid-seventeenth century, the Great Fifth Dalai Lama ordered the construction of a new Potala on the same spot as the former king's palace, with work continuing for fifty consecutive years, progressing beyond the life of the Great Fifth. Its massive size astounded Pema and Lhamo. How, they wondered, did such a building exist?

For nearly thirteen centuries, the Potala had represented the seat of Tibet's governance and later the winter home for the ruling Dalai Lama. From its dominating position, this massive structure reminded Lhamo of what had once represented Tibet in the stories she had heard all her life. Without a Dalai Lama, monks, and Tibetan government officials to fill its enormous interior, the Potala has today become nothing more than a piece of Tibet's history, a magnificent but empty palace brimming with echoes of the past, and the noise of curious tourists mingling with murmured prayers from Tibetan pilgrims.

With no modern labor skills to speak of, the girls soon found themselves eking out an existence alongside many of their Tibetan counterparts. Among the large number of Chinese occupants in the city, Lhamo often felt like a stranger in her own land, yet she felt no ill will toward the Chinese. She could see they were people whose circumstances were not much different than hers. Over time, the girls took many odd jobs: cooking and serving food at a Chinese restaurant, washing cars, watering plants throughout the city—they even tried running their own restaurant. They lived frugally and saved their hard-earned money.

Both learned to speak the Lhasa dialect of the Tibetan language and enough Mandarin to get along in the now-Chinese-dominated city. For two years they worked and saved, until finally they had enough to pay a guide to navigate them through the mountains and into Nepal. They would not make the trek together, however; Pema would follow the wishes of her aunt and leave with members of her own family weeks before Lhamo.

With nearly 4,000 yuan tucked away, enough money to embark on the next part of her journey to see His Holiness, all Lhamo needed was a guide. Finding one meant accessing an illegal network, shrouded in secrecy. Numerous men guide Tibetans out of the country; some do it only for financial gain, charging exorbitant fees per person. Others are motivated by a sense of altruism, coupled with the opportunity to earn large sums of money—one trip can net several thousand yuan, enough to live on for a year.

Guiding Tibetans across the Himalayas is a risky way to earn a living, as crossing from Tibet to Nepal through the Himalayas is not only treacherous due to the climate and terrain, but the territory is also well patrolled by allies of the PRC, which has made it illegal for Tibetans to cross into Nepal or India through the mountains. Aside from unpredictable and extreme weather conditions and the challenging terrain and physical dangers of high mountain passes, guides and escapees face being captured and jailed, tortured, and even shot and killed enroute. Chinese border police vigilantly patrol the passes, searching for Tibetans headed for Nepal, and to help crack down on what it considers illegal crossings both before and after they occur, China has also enlisted the Nepalese military to assist in patrolling Nepal's borders and towns. It also pays informants in remote villages near the routes, where opportunists are willing to trade secrets for cash.

Through discreet investigation, Lhamo tapped into the underground network of guides, which eventually yielded a contact. In a small Chinese restaurant, she met with a representative of the *snakeheads* who would take her through the mountains into Nepal. In hushed tones, they discussed preliminary details of the cost and length of the journey. She was instructed to pack lightly, bringing tsampa mixed with butter and cheese, dried meat, an extra pair of shoes and socks, a blanket or sleeping bag, a warm coat, and minimal personal effects—if any.

"If you are serious, you must make a deposit today; we will call you when the time comes." Unhaltingly, Lhamo slipped 500 yuan across the table as a commitment to her intentions. "Be ready when we call; everything should be packed and waiting to go. You will have to be quick. There will be a car waiting for you; be ready and tell no one."

With the guide arranged and her bag packed, she waited anxiously for several days. Late one night, the call finally came. The voice on the other end instructed her that a vehicle would pick her up in thirty minutes at a specific location. She must not be late. Grabbing her backpack and donning her sheepskin chuba, Lhamo hurried out into the night, found the waiting car, and, without hesitation or fear, climbed inside. She and the driver exchanged one-word—"Lhamo"—to confirm she was the person he had been sent to retrieve; beyond that, the seriousness of their undertaking committed them to silence. After a short distance, the car stopped, and she was instructed to get into another vehicle. About an hour's drive out of Lhasa, the driver stopped at a large, tarp-covered truck parked near a monastery. She was instructed to get into the back of the truck, and obediently Lhamo did as she was told. To her surprise, nearly sixty people were already packed into the truck bed like sardines. Over the next few minutes, people moved closer together and made room for new additions that continued to arrive out of the darkness.

When a total of seventy-five people had assembled, some were none too happy at the high risk of such a large group passing through the mountains. Fanned by tension and growing fear, tempers flared. Arguments and accusations of being cheated ensued. Outside the truck, a tall and imposing man stepped forward authoritatively: Kunga, who hailed from Kham, was a former member of the Chinese People's Armed Police (PAP). During his tenure, he had patrolled the same mountains he now led Tibetans through to make his living; his military experience and training made him an ideal guide. Poking his head into the back of the truck, he demanded silence. "I know what I'm doing; stop complaining or get out." Silence descended immediately among the disgruntled. With his authoritative demeanor and gruff language, Kunga was a hard man to argue with. He then commanded, "No more talking." Silence dropped over the group as the truck's tarpaulin cover was pulled closed, enveloping the escapees in darkness. The large vehicle rumbled off into the night, led and followed convoy-style by several cars, each keeping a reasonable distance. Kunga and his guiding companion, Dorjee, traveled separately, supplying both men with the ability to deny any involvement should the truck be stopped and searched.

The escapees, many of them school-aged children, traveled in complete silence, as instructed. Children were often sent to India to receive an education in one of the Tibetan-run schools. The children would make the journey accompanied by siblings, older family members, or a trusted Lama—rarely with parents—and most would never see their parents again. In a communal society like Tibet's, it was understood that other adults would care for the children.

Lhamo dozed off and on as the truck bounced away from Lhasa. They traveled east along the Lhasa River—also known as the Kyi Chu River—and then abruptly turned north, opposite to the direction in which the escapees wanted to go. In the dark confines of the truck, it was impossible to know where they were. As the truck lumbered along, the road grew increasingly rough, and the children and older adults grunted and groaned with each rut. When the truck ground to a halt and the tarp was thrown aside, Kunga's face appeared, ordering everyone to get out. They were now in the Yerpa Valley, ten miles northeast of Lhasa, and had driven a further six miles to the limestone caves of the Drak Yerpa. Here, the escaping Tibetans were to pose as pilgrims at one of Tibet's historically significant spiritual sites. The guides wanted to quell any chance of suspicion in case they'd been followed out of Lhasa.

The Drak Yerpa is home to some of Tibet's oldest meditation caves, some predating Buddhism. For a day they toured the site, praying, prostrating, circumambulating the stupas, and walking through the ruins of the former monastery. The *"pilgrims"* were happy for the opportunity to pray there, but as dusk descended, they piled back into the cramped vehicle. From Drak Yerpa, the truck made its way southwest on the Friendship Highway along the Kyi Chu River, and then further south along the Tsangpo River. Mercifully, the road was mostly smooth, and the cold air provided relief from the claustrophobic conditions. They traveled for over eight hours before coming to an abrupt halt at a military checkpoint just outside of Shigatse. The nervous escapees hunkered down in fearful silence; Lhamo listened intently to voices speaking Mandarin outside the truck. At any moment, she feared Chinese soldiers with guns would lift the tarp and her journey would be over. Instead, the engine rumbled to life, and they moved on.

A hundred miles later, the truck veered off the highway before the military checkpoint in Lhatse, a small town 200 miles due north of Nepal's border. The large truck would be conspicuous in the small city and unlikely to make it through the checkpoint without being searched. In the early-morning hours, the driver found a hidden ravine in which to park the truck for a few hours of rest. At nightfall, they started off once again, only to stop a short time later. It was the end of the road for vehicle passage. Everyone spilled from the truck into the fierce winds of the harsh landscape above the tree line. Lhamo attempted to stretch her body, but the bracing, sand-laden gusts forced her to turn her back and draw her chuba up around her neck for warmth.

To decrease their chance of detection, they would trek mostly in the dark of night at dizzying altitudes above the villages scattered in the valleys and foothills. The cover of darkness was a protective necessity against the spying eyes of villagers and border patrols. Following a dry creek bed, the group grappled for footing in the dark. Faint beams of flashlights from a few among them did little to illuminate the terrain.

Those first hours were relatively uneventful as the escapees adjusted to traveling by foot in the dark. Some people knew each other, but most were complete strangers—men, women, and children of various ages and physical abilities. All were just as determined as Lhamo to reach India. What little water they had with them was gone by morning, and the next water source was still a day and a half away. Hardship had begun. Without water to drink or use to prepare tsampa, thirst and hunger quickly set in. Children whined and cried. A few days in, blisters formed on feet clad in cheap sneakers and faux hiking boots, and two people with injured ankles were left behind with Dorjee, who would follow at a slower pace. Kunga was now the only guide for more than seventy people.

Kunga planned to take them through the pass at Mt. Cho Oyu. The mountain is well known among mountain climbers of Mt. Everest and is the sixth-highest mountain in the world. Cho Oyu means "Turquoise Goddess" in Tibetan, and Lhamo had heard many stories about it. She knew there was a large open area called the Nangpa La Pass directly to the west of the peak. From her vantage point now, though large, she knew the snow-covered mountains were days away. The terrain around them seemed lifeless; at over 14,000 feet in elevation, it was devoid of trees, brown, dusty, and barren, like a vast sea of lifeless land reaching for gleaming white ahead. Tough brownish-green grasses and small shrubs poked up occasionally; otherwise, there was nothing, except mountains in all directions, far off in the distance.

It wasn't long before even the lightest backpacks seemed unbearably heavy in the unrelenting terrain. People started leaving clothes and belongings, which lay scattered behind them. Lhamo was strong and accustomed to physical exertion, but even for her the continual ascent and descent was a strain. She repeatedly stumbled over scrabble and clumps of alpine grasses made invisible by the pitch-black night. *I can go further, I must go further; there is no choice now*, she told herself repeatedly.

In September, the average high temperature in the region is below freezing, even during the day. The bright sunlight provided little warmth, and resting during the day was so uncomfortable Lhamo never slept soundly. No one else in the group fared any better. In particular, the children had difficulty resting after such punishing nighttime treks; without sleeping bags of their own, they would sleep with a generous adult to keep warm. Accustomed to hard conditions but not to being away from home, the children required assistance and tending from all the adults now making their way through the unforgiving landscape. Frostbite was a constant concern in glacial conditions, and in past treks, it had not been uncommon for people to reach India with blackened toes, fingers, or feet. Even worse, some had fallen into unseen crevasses and been lost forever. Lhamo was fully aware of the possible dangers that might befall her, yet she clung to the faith in her destiny and kept moving forward, scanning the ground at her feet and occasionally the white in the distance ahead. But as the days and nights wore on, her resolve was repeatedly tested.

Night after night, grueling hour after grueling hour, Mt. Everest and Mt. Cho Oyu's snowy peaks, lit by the moon, grew larger. But by the time they reached the treeless Tingri Salt Plains, Lhamo felt she was living an unending bad dream. The four-day trek they had been promised had turned into ten, and food supplies were nearly exhausted. The hunger that had growled in her stomach in the first few days was now a discomforting quiet; exhaustion clung like a pervasive weight. Sometimes she wanted to just lie down and sleep, but somehow her feet kept moving her forward.

The night before they entered the Nangpa La Glacier, which would take them south into Nepal, Kunga instructed the travelers to combine their remaining food supplies, mostly tsampa and a few bits of dried cheese and meat, to make a soup to share. Although it was thin and meager, it would have to hold them through the next day's trek across the high pass. Nepal's border and relative safety lay just beyond—they were so close to the end. The Nangpa La Pass has been used for centuries as a trade and pilgrimage route and is the most direct passage through the mountains. Above the Nangpa La Glacier and below the lower curve of the Gyabrag Glacier, the pass is approximately a half-mile wide and 19,000 feet in altitude. As far back as the days of the Silk Road, traders traversed the wide expanse of the pass, which served as the bridge between Tibet and Nepal. Mt. Cho Oyu's Advance Base Camp (ABC) overlooks the pass from the north. At ABC, mountain climbers begin their altitude acclimation prior to climbing to three progressively higher base camps and the final ascension of the nearly 27,000-foot Cho Oyu peak.

Skirting the western edge of Mt. Cho Oyu's base camps in the early-morning light on September 30, 2006, Lhamo took in the view of the colorful dome tents dotting the white landscape, and the flags of numerous nations rippling in the wind. Kunga had decided that moving through the pass in the daytime would be relatively safe. After days in muted-hued landscapes and darkness, the view was like a mirage. Lhamo remembers the way the tents, in almost every color, stood out against the white snow and blue sky overhead. "I felt less alone somehow, like we were closer to our goal, and my attitude was much better on seeing all the colors and people." Like the rest of the group, she was weak and eager to reach Nepal. Hunger pushed some members of the group boldly toward the foreigners' camp in search of something to abate the gnawing in their stomachs and bolster shaky limbs. With climbers from nineteen countries and a large population of Sherpas and Tibetans working with the expedition companies, they would be able to blend in as long as they avoided the Chinese camps. Though the sight of the camp lifted Lhamo's spirits, she did not want to walk among so many strangers and stayed where she was. With the Chinese nearby, it was a risky move.

All along the trek, the faster-moving people in the group had left the slower ones trailing behind—mostly children and the adults tending them. Nangpa La would be no different. After entering the pass, a group of twenty surged ahead, making their way up the wide, steep, snow-covered terrain. At 19,000 feet in elevation, it was a painful slog, and Lhamo fell behind with the slower group. She plodded through the deep snow, staying silent except for the labor of her breath. At these extreme elevations, the lungs and brain can fill with liquid, resulting in life-threatening pulmonary and cerebral edema. Even though Tibetans have physically adapted to high-altitude conditions over thousands of years,[1] the Nangpa La Pass was a beast, and Lhamo struggled for breath as she focused on putting one foot in front of the other. Weakened from days without proper nourishment or rest, combined with the punishing journey through the terrain of the Himalayas and now this last climb through the pass, Lhamo felt lightheaded. But she couldn't stop now; where would she go, and what would she do? Turn around and go home? No. There was nothing left to do but continue moving forward, regardless of her discomfort.

"We never should have gone into the pass early in the morning; it was foolish. All those days we had walked at night kept us safe. I don't know why he [Kunga] took us there in the morning." In hindsight, Lhamo thinks maybe Kunga thought a camp filled with foreigners would be a deterrent to border police taking adverse action against the escapees. For that is what they were in the eyes of the Chinese: illegals escaping China. Though most of the group were near collapse from hunger and fatigue, Kunga must have decided it was worth the risk, given the proximity to Nepal's border. It wasn't that he didn't care; there were simply few decisions in his line of work that guaranteed a positive outcome.

Several minutes after Lhamo entered the mouth of the pass, the silence was shattered by loud blasts that ricocheted off the mountains. "I thought the men with the tents were lighting firecrackers, and I looked up to see what was happening. When people near me started yelling 'Hide, hide!' I knew it wasn't firecrackers. I couldn't see the guns, but I could hear them." The group had been discovered and was being fired upon from the ridge above.

From her position at the beginning of the pass, she couldn't see or be seen by the Chinese border patrol. However, the twenty people ahead of her were being shot at as they struggled through the snow and up the steep incline. Panic seized everyone around her; backpacks were hurriedly flung to the ground like trash and people began running in all directions. Lhamo watched this play out, almost frozen with fear. She threw herself to the ground, praying to go unnoticed as the sound of gunfire reverberated through the pass. From her small backpack, she took out special packets of barley blessed by Tibetan Lamas. Believing in the protective forces they contained, she slipped them into her pocket. Behind her, a man told her not to move, or she would be killed. "Better to be arrested!" he shouted. Momentarily paralyzed by fear and panic, she didn't know if she should stay or run. For what seemed like a long time, her panicked mind flitted among her choices: stay put, run, hide. Repeatedly, she cycled through the thoughts in mere seconds. Without making a conscious decision, adrenaline took over her body, forcing her to run, as fast as she could, across the snow and away from the gunfire. Lhamo surged forward on hands and knees, half-crawling, half-running. Suddenly puffs of snow sprayed into the air around her as bullets landed within inches. Her mind screamed at her—*faster, faster!* Panicked cries squeezed from her throat as she struggled across the snow. Behind her she could hear one of the girls following her, yelling, "They're killing people!" Ahead, Lhamo spied a woman from the group beckoning to her from a small snow cave under an outcropping of rock below the ridge from which the gunfire originated; she ran toward the woman and quickly slipped into its icy cover, safe from the hail of bullets.

Two women were in the cave with Lhamo, and for the next few hours, they huddled together, unsure of what was happening to the remaining members of the group. After the gunfire and shouting stopped, the silence was deafening. In their small pocket of snow and ice, they listened intently for sound, any sound at all—the crunch of snow, voices, anything that signaled safety or danger. There was nothing but their ragged breath and weeping, muffled by the snow cave. As the sun continued to rise in the sky, Lhamo wondered how they would get out of the pass unnoticed. The intensity of the sun began melting the little pocket of ice where they hid, and their clothes were getting wet. Concerned about freezing once the sun went down, Lhamo knew they had to keep themselves warm. "We will die if we stay here; we must leave soon," Lhamo warned them.

"It is too dangerous out there! We can't!" One of the girls hadn't stopped crying since they entered the cave.

Sternly, Lhamo advised, "We have no food, no water, and our clothes will freeze tonight. Crying won't help us now; you must stop." Lhamo was terrified too, but she knew continuing to hide spelled another kind of danger.

Summoning all her courage, Lhamo ventured to the opening and quickly peered out. All she saw was a white expanse. Chancing a second look, she lingered to scan more thoroughly. No one with a gun was moving around out there; in fact, there didn't appear to be anyone at all.

"I think they are gone now."

"Are you sure? Look again." Once again, Lhamo moved to the opening, lingering to carefully scan what she could of the area before poking her head farther out. She tried to see the ridge above, but couldn't. She crawled a foot out of the cave and saw maroon fabric fluttering against the snow a few hundred feet ahead. She popped back into the cave.

"There is no one moving out there, but I see a maroon robe ahead. Who was ahead of us?"

The women thought in silence for a few moments, each replaying the morning's events in their minds. "I think Ani Kelsang was ahead in the first group, and they were going very fast when the guns started. Is it a backpack you see?" one of the girls asked.

"Let me look again." Now Lhamo crawled out as far as she dared, looking in every direction as she went. The pass was deathly quiet; she ventured farther. Were her eyes betraying her? It looked like a body up ahead; it was too big to be a backpack. Sometimes it appeared the body was moving—Lhamo couldn't be sure. Back in the cave, Lhamo whispered, "I think it is a body, maybe 100 feet from here. Sometimes it seems to move, and then it seems very still. I am not sure what is happening, but there is no one else around, and it is very quiet."[2]

Lhamo continued to urge the women to leave the cave and finish crossing the broad expanse of the Nangpa La Pass, or else they would freeze in a few hours. The three quietly argued. Lhamo cautioned that while the cover of darkness would protect them, the pass would be treacherous once the melted snow turned to ice, and staying in the cave overnight would surely equal freezing to death. "We have to take the chance before the sun goes down. We can't stay here; it is too dangerous." After much discourse, her companions relented; they would leave their hideout. If captured, at least they would be alive. With the Nepal border only one or two days' walk away, they had to risk being caught to get out of the pass.

On hands and knees, they made their way along the path and straight to the maroon fabric. A body lay sprawled in the snow. It was Ani Kelsang. None of them could crawl past without knowing if she was alive or dead. Reaching her body, Lhamo paused for a moment and looked into the young nun's face—and her open, lifeless eyes. "Om mani padme hung"; she breathed the prayer out of her mouth as if trying to will Ani back to life. Under any other circumstance, there would be prayers and ritual, but now all they could do was continue up the steep pass, out of sight, their tears dropping to the snow.

Rising to their feet at the top of the pass, the three women made their way on as dusk set in. The danger and terror of the pass was behind them for the moment. Lhamo and her companions scanned the ground for signs of tracks and eventually picked up a trail made by those who had managed to escape the rain of bullets. Exhausted, cold, and hungry, they continued on and on in the darkness, barely able to see where their feet were treading. Eventually, the snow surrendered to rocky tundra, desolate and boulder-strewn. When they reached a river, Lhamo fished the last bits of dried meat from her pocket and shared them with her companions.

As if the day's events hadn't drained every ounce of energy from them, they now had a river to cross. Waist-deep and glacial-fed, it was treacherous at any time of day. In the darkness and without knowing how to swim, Lhamo had every reason to worry. She had forded rivers many times in the past, but this time she was at a pronounced disadvantage. Her second pair of shoes were splitting apart, and finding purchase on slippery rocks in the frigid waters seemed a dubious undertaking. Summoning up all the courage they could muster, the three grasped tightly one another's hands as they entered the water. Stumbling and slipping, they made their way slowly over slick rocks and through the icy current. Lhamo reached the bank, pulled herself up, then turned to help the others. Freezing but safe, they rested long enough to catch their breath.

As one danger passed, another took its place. Their sodden clothes and shoes began to freeze. As they stumbled over the rocks, feet that were sore, cut, and blistered were now freezing inside the remains of icy shoes. Every step was more painful than the last as their stiffened clothes scraped against their freezing flesh. Pushed to the brink of hypothermia, Lhamo wisely refused to let her companions rest, even though they repeatedly begged to stop. Moving was their only hope for survival. They had to stay active to generate the only heat available to their freezing bodies until the morning sun could warm them. Only when the sun began to rise did they dare attempt sleep.

As the sun reached its full height a few short hours later, they woke up disoriented, unable to find the path they had traversed. Wandering in confusion for several minutes, they found the tracks made by others ahead of them and hurried along as fast as they could, hoping to catch up. From the high altitude and icy snow, the three women eventually descended into the mile-wide Bhote Koshi Valley on the border of Nepal and Tibet, a sparse desert of sand, rock, scrub bushes, and rust-colored hillsides. Even at 12,000 feet, the extra oxygen lifted some of the fog from their brains and gave them a surge of energy.

The mountains sloping to the valley were covered with altitude-stunted pines, short grasses, and heather fading from summer-green to rusty browns. As daylight began to fade to evening hues, they found themselves at the mighty Bhote Koshi River. They crossed a rickety wooden bridge where the river diminishes to small pools and streams, and headed toward the tiny two-roomed Arya Guest House. Built of stone, this was the first of several safe houses in Nepal where they would, at last, have food and rest, and hopefully find Kunga and the remaining group.

Shocked to see the bedraggled girls enter the guesthouse, everyone gathered around. "Where are the others? Where are the children?" Lhamo didn't have answers—only that Ani Kelsang lay dead on the pass. The fates of the remaining group members were unknown. Equally disquieting was that the guide was missing and most likely arrested. Kunga had been in the group behind Lhamo when the gunfire started, pointing the way to the adults, saying he would stay behind with the children. Too young and weak to outrun their pursuers, the group assumed that most of the children were now in the custody of the Chinese police.

For the first time since leaving Lhasa, Lhamo ate solid food and drank hot butter tea. The keeper of the guesthouse charged a small amount of money for the food and accommodations; this was, after all, his only livelihood. Having walked during the day in the bright sun glaring off the snow, many were suffering from snow blindness and couldn't keep their eyes open without a flood of painful tears. Since Lhamo and her companions had crossed much of the snowy expanse at dusk, their eyes were unaffected. Using an ancient remedy that blocked out the light and allowed the eyes to heal, Lhamo made a paste of butter mixed with tsampa, applying it gently over the eyelids of her companions. Although everyone in the group had been strangers just a few weeks ago, now they shared the burden of their situation, and many mourned for their missing compatriots, especially Ani Kelsang Namtso, dead so young, so unnecessarily.

On the second day, Kunga finally showed up. He explained that he had hidden when the shooting had begun, and was unable to help the children and handful of adults without risking his safety. As the panicked group had dispersed in many directions, Kunga slipped into a tent in the Filipino camp, where he had hidden among packs from the prying eyes of the People's Armed Police. He later made his escape with the help of the Sherpas working for the Filipino climbing group. He was sorry to report that the remaining children had been arrested. But he was happy to see that so many of the group had made it to the safe house.

When Dorjee showed up a day later, claiming he had lost the two people he had stayed behind to help, Kunga flew into a rage. "How could you lose two people? All you had to do was look after two people!" Tempers flared as the guides continued to argue. Before coming to physical blows, one of the monks intervened. They had not reached true safety yet, and there was no time for fighting.

Rest and food energized the group to continue, following the valley farther into Nepal as they headed to the next safe house. Landslides from the

Glacial and Early Holocene Age nearly 13,000 years ago created a barren moonscape that served as a sort of highway for Sherpas carrying goods back and forth to the climbing camps at Everest and Cho Oyu. During peak climbing season, men and women would carry huge bundles and baskets on their backs, held by large straps across their foreheads, trudging along the stark landscape to deliver all sorts of food, beverages, and gear to the foreigners climbing the high mountains. Lhamo now understood how the climbers had so much gear and food in their possession.

Once again crossing the churning Bhote Koshi River, this time farther down and via a high metal bridge, Lhamo stopped to peek over the edge. The river was a torrent of frothing white water. Looming above was a painted mural of Padmasambhava, the eighth-century Buddhist master and a deity steeped in mythos by Tibetans, Indians, and Nepali Buddhists, painted on a vast expanse of flat stone. To Lhamo, in that moment, even a mural on rocks lifted her spirits and reminded her she had made it through the worst of her travails. Her destination was close at hand.

Reaching another safe house, Kunga quietly consulted with a man who worked for the Tibetan Refugee Reception Center (TRRC).[3] Carefully, the man recorded each member of the group's name, age, and place of birth to pass on to the refugee center in Kathmandu. Though the travelers were not entirely out of danger, and they still had many miles to traverse, Lhamo couldn't help but feel a small sense of relief.

Like so many in the group, Lhamo's shoes were worn to shreds. At the request of the TRRC contact, dozens of cheap shoes were brought to the safe house to see them through the last leg of their journey. The next day, the group worked their way through the Namche Bazaar, famous as the Sherpa and trekking capital of the world. On the hunt for more supplies and food to travel with, the group separated into smaller squads and moved as quickly as possible without rousing suspicion. Filled with Nepali officials, many on the lookout for escaping Tibetans just like Lhamo, it was a dangerous place to tarry too long. Kunga led them off the main path to descend the mountainside, away from Namche. Heavily forested, the trails provided cover, and the sweet smell of pine and woods filled Lhamo with a sense of well-being. Nearing the village of Lukla, Kunga once again led the group down and away from the settlement, home to the most dangerous airport in the world. At a 9,000-foot altitude and with a 1,500-foot runway that ends in a sheer drop, the Tenzing-Hillary Airport is the quickest route from Kathmandu to Everest. Given this strategic proximity to Everest and thus its importance to the climbing industry's economy, the airport is well guarded by the Nepali military. Lukla's small village, crowded with tourists during the climbing season, is also well policed. Avoiding any chance of trouble at this point was paramount; the group had made it too far to be apprehended now.

Slowly, they descended into the humid, oppressive heat of a bamboo forest. Acclimated to a cold, arid climate, the ragtag group struggled along with rivulets of sweat seeping through heavy clothing. Tying her sheepskin chuba at the waist failed to provide Lhamo the relief she sought and, little by little, clothes were peeled off and carried. Once they were safely past Lukla, Kunga led them back up the mountain, where they waited for a bus bound southward for a Tibetan settlement in the area. To her horror, Lhamo discovered giant black leeches clinging to her ankles and legs and making their way up her arms. Everyone in the group suffered the same fate. Careful not to kill any, they peeled each leech off, one by one, and placed them in the bushes. Tibetans hold the belief that every living thing could have been one's mother in a past life, so even a leech must be handled carefully.

The final stop was a safe house near Kotari. Five days had passed since the shooting at the Nangpa La Pass; Lhamo knew they weren't completely safe, yet the tension she had been carrying for days was beginning to slowly seep from her body. Several hours later, she and the others boarded a bus to Kathmandu and the safety of the TRRC. A huge grin spread across her face as she climbed aboard the large vehicle, which she said was "very beautiful and like a dream." Riding in style aboard an air-conditioned and plush-seated bus in which they could curl up and sleep was a delicious treat after such a grueling experience. "I felt so much relief and knew we were all finally safe; for the first time in many days, I could relax." Only seventy miles lay between Lhamo and Kathmandu, and this time no walking was required. As the bus rumbled along the bumpy road, Lhamo curled up to sleep, but it wasn't long before she and a few others began to feel queasy.

Motion sickness was something she had never endured before, having only recently traveled by vehicle. She was frightened that something was wrong with her, especially as others began showing similar signs of distress. They vomited into tiny bags tucked into the seatbacks that Kunga and the TRRC official had shown them. Kunga assured them that this was a regular occurrence, however miserable. Sleeping was the best remedy.

Twelve long hours later, the bus rumbled to a stop in front of the iron gates of the nondescript TRRC. Inside the courtyard, Lhamo descended from the bus, along with forty-three of the original members, including three children, who had set out from Lhasa twenty-two days earlier. The sun was warm, and Lhamo took note of the many Tibetans relaxing in the courtyard as children played around them. How long had they been here, she wondered, and had they suffered the same fate as she and her group had?

Unbeknownst to Lhamo and the others in the group, the shooting on the pass and the death of Ani Kelsang had made news around the world, and a great deal of attention would soon descend upon them. Romanian mountain climber and cameraman Sergiu Matei had filmed the entire shooting incident on Nangpa La. When the first shots had rung out across the pass, Matei had instinctively run for his camera. From his vantage point on the ridge above the pass, he'd had a clear view of Ani Kelsang falling in the snow. She had struggled to move forward a few times and then had lain motionless as the rest of her group struggled up the pass, away from the bullets. In addition to capturing Kelsang's shooting, Matei had also discovered Choedon, another member of Lhamo's group, hiding in a latrine under a bag of used toilet paper. He had filmed Choedon as well, and then later helped him escape to safety. In the meantime, Matei and others on the mountain had alerted the outside world to what had happened. By the time Lhamo's group had arrived at the TRRC, journalists the world over were clamoring for interviews. A young woman named Dolma, the best friend of Ani Kelsang—along with Choedon, whose latrine story was all over the news—was thrust into the center of the media melee. Lhamo was thankful she did not have to endure so much attention.

Although the initial flurry of media attention was overwhelming, at least it wasn't directed solely at her, and she felt safe in Kathmandu, being able to rest and eat. At night in her bunk bed, her thoughts turned to Ani Kelsang lying in the white snow, her maroon robe fluttering in the wind. It easily could have been Lhamo lying there. Sometimes her mind replayed the sound of bullets hitting the snow all around her as she scrambled for safety, and these thoughts drifted into her dreams, torturing her sleep.

Processing for refugees at the TRRC normally required two or three months. However, amid fear that the Chinese would intervene and attempt to force the return of the highly publicized Nangpa La group, the processing was rushed through in just one week. With the assistance of the United Nations High Command for Refugees (UNHCR), the group would reach India safely. Lhamo was grateful as she boarded a bus bound for New Delhi and the Tibetan settlement of Majnu Ka Tilla. There, they were to rest a few more days before making the journey to Dharamsala and the Dalai Lama.

After resting in New Delhi's Tibetan settlement, Lhamo and the remaining members of her group boarded the overnight bus to Dharamsala, arriving in the little town of McLeodganj in the early hours of dawn. Lhamo was filled with excitement, curiosity, and a deep sense of gratitude that her wish to meet His Holiness was just around the corner. In New Delhi, she had already had a glimpse of life in India. It was much warmer than she had expected, and the cooler air in the mountains was a relief from the stifling heat of Delhi. She had imagined the home of His Holiness as an extraordinary and beautiful palace, just like the Potala Palace in Lhasa. She was shocked to find a simple, dusty town in the hills with narrow, pockmarked dirt roads; wandering cows defecating in the streets and eating trash; disabled beggars on the side of the road; and a very humble temple and home to the Dalai Lama that wasn't visible from every area of town, like the

Potala. At first, she found the incongruity challenging to fathom. Over time, she learned what it meant to live as an exile, a stateless refugee with nothing: no state, no identification, no money, no voice, and no power.

Tibetans who arrive in Dharamsala from Tibet always have a group audience with His Holiness the Fourteenth Dalai Lama. Usually, he offers words of encouragement and comfort to ease the hardship they have endured. This particular group of escapees had suffered so much, and he understood the scars each would carry throughout their lives. As always, he encouraged each person not to allow anger to darken their hearts, telling them that forgiveness and compassion would help heal the wounds. His words acknowledged the details of their hardship, including the death of one of their sisters.

He blessed each as they filed past him with their hands clasped in prayer and heads bowed in reverence. In the ancient blessing tradition, he took the long white silk khata scarf offerings from each person and draped them over their bowed heads and onto their necks while murmuring words of encouragement. He gently held the hands of some, occasionally squeezed a shoulder with affection, or held a tear-filled face in his hands for a few moments. Overcome by the presence of the beloved leader of Tibet, there are always tears. In those brief moments, the Dalai Lama did what he could to provide solace. For Lhamo, meeting the Dalai Lama was an indescribable moment that helped ease the terror of her experience. Satisfied in reaching her destination and His Holiness, she turned her mind to what would come next.

Over the next few months, the group of escapees diverged on different paths and eventually scattered across India, Nepal, and Tibet. Some joined other family members in India, and a few even bravely returned to Tibet across the mountains, daring fate once again. The youngest were dispersed to several Tibetan-run schools located throughout India, entering the family system of the Tibetan Children's Villages (TCV), a community for the care and education of exiled children. Parting from one another reminded Lhamo of how much they had endured together. From strangers to friends bonded by a journey few could comprehend, across the Roof of the World, where surviving the cruelty of humans was as treacherous as the perils of the highest mountains on earth. They shared an unspoken understanding and an unbreakable bond that no one else would ever truly comprehend.

Enrolled in the Tibetan Transit School, for the first time in her life Lhamo began to study how to read and write in her native Tibetan language. She also learned English and how to use a computer and studied tailoring as a trade. There was so much to learn in this strange country. Lhamo struggled, as did all the newcomers, to adjust to the culture, food, and language. Plagued with homesickness, Lhamo wanted so much to share her journey with her parents and tell them she was safe, but most of all she wanted to tell her mother what it was like to meet His Holiness. With no phone or mail system in the village nearest her parents, Lhamo could only send messages through acquaintances headed to Tibet, or with others who were digitally connected, hoping someone would eventually get word to her parents. Also, like the majority of Tibetans who reach India, she became sick—likely from water and food-borne bacteria—and the illness impacted her ability to adjust to the point that she quit school for a time. All put together, illness, homesickness, and displacement grew into a depression that simmered below the surface. At one time, leaving Tibet had seemed like such a carefree move toward an unknown and exciting adventure. That adventure she had dreamed about for so long ended up being nothing like what she had imagined. Lhamo hadn't counted on the challenges of adjusting to a new life in a strange world and the almost constant ache in her mind and heart for her home. For the first year especially, homesickness and illness overshadowed her newfound independence. She doubted her decision to leave home constantly, and wanted to apologize to her parents for not having listened to them.

Eventually, Lhamo made a life for herself in McLeodganj. She found work as a tailor, continued to study English, and made new friends. She settled into her little cement room, with its pink walls and the constant hum of the TV. Twice a day, someone would shout, "Chooh! Chooh!" (Water, water!). Grabbing her water buckets, Lhamo would stand in line with her neighbors, sharing idle gossip while waiting for the daily water ration. She was also able to finally talk with her parents, thanks to the growth of cell phone services across India and China. What they could say was limited to personal health, weather, work, and a few details about family members. Politics, China's government, the Dalai Lama, and Lhamo's escape were never discussed out of fear that their conversations were being monitored. Lhamo had to be satisfied in hearing her parents' voices and knowing they were alive and healthy. Regretfully, Lhamo couldn't share the details of what it had been like to meet Kundun with her mother.

Lhamo learned that saying goodbye to friends and family was a way of life in the tiny hilltop town. McLeodganj and other Tibetan settlements in India are transient; no one wants to stay permanently in a constant state of limbo, exiled from home and family; an opportunity to go abroad or return to Tibet is on everyone's mind. Lhamo said farewell to many friends during her years in India. Hiding her sadness with an expression of good wishes, she saw her friends off time and again at the bus station. Each time she draped a khata scarf over a friend, wishing them a safe journey, she also fought the stings of loss, regret, and sadness.

After nearly a decade living in India, Lhamo received her own khatas and wishes for a safe journey from a group of friends. Bound for Australia, a new husband, a new life, and eventually children, she said goodbye to India, to the Dalai Lama, to her friends, and to the high snow mountains of the Dhauladhar Range. One day, she hoped to return to Tibet as an Australian citizen. Then she would see her beloved homeland and the passage of time in her parents' graying hair and bent spines. She would introduce her children to all their relatives and the green pastures and high mountains of Lhamo's Tibet. She would find that Tibet had changed a great deal since her childhood, in part because she had changed. Her perception of the world would be broader and deeper, and she would no longer be an ignorant girl milking dri and churning butter.

Lhamo had traveled a long distance since that 700-mile journey from her nomadic life in eastern Tibet to the holy city of Lhasa. The process of transcending the trauma of Nangpa La may never be complete; the sound of automatic gunfire and sprays of snow as she crawled through the pass will always be with her. Even now, when she sees mountains full of snow or soldiers armed with guns, or hears cracks of thunder, her heart races as memories of that terrible day on the 19,000-foot pass rush back to her. Despite the pain of the past, Lhamo has found a deep sense of gratitude for the life she has lived and the one she is living now.

Lhamo emigrated to Australia in 2015, where she joined her husband. She now has two beautiful daughters and is happy and safe in a democratic country that has provided her with citizenship. She is no longer a stateless person with no future. Lhamo has not returned to Tibet… yet.

THE NANGPA LA INCIDENT

The base camp at Mt. Cho Oyu provides an amphitheater-like view of the Nangpa La Pass. Climbers who rose early on the morning of September 30, 2006 were witness to something many found unthinkable, and the experience continues to haunt some. Earlier that morning, only fifteen miles away, officers at the military base were notified that Tibetans had been spotted in what appeared to be an escape. Scrambling into trucks, the officers were quickly on their way to carry out an order to stop fleeing Tibetans from leaving the country. The *Wujing*, the paramilitary wing of the People's Armed Police (PAP), was under orders to arrest or shoot anyone caught escaping through the pass to Nepal.

When the shooting on the Nangpa La Pass began infiltrating global news circuits, China issued a statement refuting the murder accusations. Chinese leaders concocted a story that would later be proved false. The government-owned news station Xinhua reported, "the frontier soldiers were forced to defend themselves [against attack] and injured two stowaways." The statement went on to say that one person died due to an oxygen shortage and another injured party was under treatment at a local hospital. The Chinese didn't know at that point, however, of the existence of Sergiu Matei's video footage, as well as numerous still photographs from other climbers, which provided irrefutable proof of Kelsang's murder and of the border patrol blatantly opening fire on Tibetans who had been running away from the shooters.

The climbing website MountEverest.net initially stalled releasing the news of the event, but two days after the shooting, it decided to release details about what the climbers had witnessed. Ten days later, Matei's video was uploaded to MountEverest.net. Nearly two weeks after the shooting, Romania's PRO TV interviewed Matei and aired his footage. Very quickly, news outlets around the world, including CNN and the BBC, picked up the film and began airing it internationally. The video provided a direct contradiction of China's account of events, ignited a media frenzy, and triggered a political firestorm aimed directly at China. Between eyewitness statements and the video footage, it was evident that the escaping Tibetans had posed zero threat to anyone. Though the incident received global media and political attention, in the end, China was never held to account by any governmental entity, including the UN Human Rights Council. China would recant its previous statement, saying that one person in the group died of a gunshot wound. In time, the event disappeared from the media and faded into the world of past human tragedies.

Thirty-two of the original group of seventy-five Tibetans—many of them children—were arrested on Nangpa La by Chinese border soldiers, and some were eventually released back to their families in Tibet. However, seventeen remain unaccounted for. Later, one of the teenaged captives reported having been tortured during intense interrogations focused on his associations with the Dalai Lama and the Tibetan-exiled government, and having been put in a labor camp. He was eventually released and again made his way over the mountains to Nepal, this time successfully. One man was shot twice in the legs and was later taken into custody. His whereabouts are unknown. Ani Kelsang was the only confirmed death.

Were it not for the quick actions of Sergiu Matei, the outside world would not have witnessed the murder of the Tibetan nun Ani Kelsang, shot in the back while fleeing up the steep slope by Chinese border patrol from the ridge overlooking the pass. They would not have seen Tibetans falling to the ground, shot in the back, shot in the legs, shot at "like dogs," as Matei is heard to say in his video recording. The world would not have seen people who posed zero threat to anyone fleeing for their lives from gunfire.

Why the Chinese feel it's necessary to prevent Tibetans from leaving the country—to shoot or arrest them—is a question I've been asked many times. I try to imagine an instance in which the United States Border Patrol would shoot an American citizen walking across the border into Canada or Mexico, and an absurd picture forms in my mind. The mission of the US Border Patrol is to "detect and prevent illegal aliens, terrorists, and terrorist weapons from entering the United States and prevent illegal trafficking of people and contraband."[4] Border protection is typically focused on preventing illegal entry, not exit. In accordance with eyewitness statements, news editors and politicians in many countries found that the video footage from Nangpa La clearly refuted China's claims. The border police clearly violated the laws set forth by Article 13 of the United Nations Universal Declaration of Human Rights: "Everyone has the right to leave any country, including his own, and to return to his country."

When a government ratifies an international human rights treaty, it essentially commits to putting into place domestic measures and legislation compatible with the stated obligations and duties of the treaty. A participating state's domestic legal system, therefore, provides the principal legal protection of the rights guaranteed under international law. As one of five Permanent Members of the UN Security Council, China is a participating government in the treaty, and yet it regularly violates international law—and gets away with it.

While the incident received global media attention concerning the issues of human rights violations in Tibet, the shootings also received serious attention from several governments worldwide. On November 30, 2006, at a meeting of the UN Human Rights Council in Geneva, Switzerland, sixteen NGOs in a joint statement questioned the UN High Commissioner for Human Rights on the steps taken concerning the September 30 killing of a Tibetan in the Nangpa La Pass. The High Commissioner did not respond.

To this day, Ani Kelsang Namtso's murder remains unpunished.

CHAPTER 2

ON THE RUN

A humble farm girl from the beautiful Yarlung Valley in the Tibet Autonomous Region, Dolma is in perpetual motion. It's not a nervous, neurotic type of motion; instead, she is calm and assured. Her precise movements reveal years of experience as her deft hands string beads and tie intricate knots for malas, necklaces, and earrings. She and her second husband, Kunchok, sell jewelry from a tent stall on the side of the road in McLeodganj, India. Business is inconsistent, fluctuating with the tourist season, drying up almost completely during the cold winter months. Though she is petite, at less than five feet tall, her physical strength is impressive, as is her iron will. Straight and waist-length, her black hair is clipped neatly in a bun, her tawny skin is smooth and unlined, and a gold-covered incisor peeks out from a friendly smile. Towering over Dolma, Kunchok is handsome, charming, and boisterous, and equally as friendly and as good-natured as his wife. Both are excellent hosts in their simple home, a small cement room of no more than 100 square feet, including a tiny kitchen and an even tinier bathroom with a squat toilet, a small sink, and a very much out-of-place non-working washing machine. There is no shower or hot water, only a large blue plastic bucket with a dipper cup for washing clothes and bodies. Furnishings are minimal: a tall gray steel cabinet and a small wooden chest store clothes, and a tiny dorm-size refrigerator sits underneath a makeshift shelf for the TV and the requisite Buddhist altar. The same area where they both sleep—carpet-covered wood structures placed in an L-shape against the walls—also serves as seating during the day for guests, as well as for dining. Pillows and neatly folded comforters double as backrests.

Dolma converses in a delightful, chirping sort of banter. This she offers up to friends and customers throughout her day, yet underneath her joviality is a deep well of emotional pain. She's had a difficult life. Simmering behind twinkling eyes is regret and homesickness, and the frustration of being powerless ever since she was forced to leave her home and family in Tibet. Tears and low-level depression emerge for only the briefest of moments in the company of her husband or trusted friends. Otherwise, these are secrets kept at bay with fierce resolve.

At twenty-six, Dolma fled Tibet for India—not because she wanted to, but because she could see no other choice. It began with her first marriage. At nineteen, she married a man she loved. Even in 2002, a love marriage was unusual in her world of family-arranged matches, but the young man from a nearby village captured her heart, and both families approved of the union. Pelsang was a good man who worked hard, and Dolma was satisfied with her choice. Their first daughter was born a year after they were married; a second baby girl arrived the following year. Though Dolma adored her girls, she was done having babies. In her mind, two children were plenty.

Large families dominate Tibetan culture, partly out of necessity, as was once true for many cultures where farming and animal husbandry necessitated offspring to assist with labor. Of course, the absence of reliable birth control factored into large families, ensuring that Tibetan women had as many as ten or twelve pregnancies. Dolma had witnessed the painful births of too many women in her village—including her own thirty-seven-year-old mother, who died shortly after giving birth for the sixth time. Dolma was about four years old when both her mother and the baby died, leaving her the youngest of five siblings.

Part of the Tibet Autonomous Region (TAR), Dolma's small village, located in Lhoka Prefecture—aka Shannan Prefecture, consisted of roughly 100 families spread out across the hills and lush valleys. The prefecture covers 30,000 square miles and is fewer than 100 miles southeast of Lhasa. Bordered to the south by Bhutan and Arunachal Pradesh—India's disputed territory with China—by Shigatse to the west, and by Nyingchi to the east, Lhoka rests in the middle and lower reaches of the Yarlung Valley. With Tibetans making up approximately 98 percent of the inhabitants, Lhoka is home to Tibet's earliest agricultural land. The Yarlung Valley is famous for several reasons, not least of which is its stunning geographical beauty. Known also as the cradle of Tibetan civilization, it was here that the first Tibetan emperor, King Songtsen Gampo (d. 649 CE), was born and became one of Tibet's most influential emperors. After extending his reach across several territories—including parts of China—which unified Tibet, he moved his court north to Lhasa, where he and two of his wives are credited with the introduction of Buddhism to the culture. He is also credited with spurring the development of the Tibetan alphabet and written language, based largely on Sanskrit.

In the agriculturally rich subtropical highland valley, the weather is temperate, the soil is fertile, and the water is plentiful. Dolma's family existed on farming and bartered for the goods they could not produce; actual money was a rarity. With her husband, father, and siblings, she worked the fields, growing barley, wheat, potatoes, and peas. The family owned a few livestock, just enough to keep them in milk, butter, and cheese, and occasionally meat. The homestead was rustic, with no running water or electricity even in the twentieth century, and, typical of Tibetan architecture, it was made with rammed earth and mud. Dolma enjoyed the physicality of farming, of being productive, and, most of all, living with her family. Born and raised on the plateau, she had never known any other life and had never wished to live elsewhere. She was content with her life and wished for nothing more.

Pelsang, however, was a restless man with big dreams, and he talked at length about ways of bettering their lives. Dolma was supportive enough to avoid discord but saw very little wrong with the life they were living. Pelsang wanted a better life and a better future for their two girls, and became convinced that opening a small store in the village would be just the ticket. Fortune took a turn for his plans, or so he believed, when the Chinese government loaned enough money to start a small business. In its efforts to lift citizens out of poverty, the PRC was pumping development subsidies into many regions of China, and that included the Tibet Autonomous Region. Dolma doesn't know how, but Pelsang was able to secure one of these development loans, though the young couple had neither collateral nor a business plan, and were uneducated, with zero cash income. She is not sure how much money it was, but suggested maybe 400,000 yuan, which seems very unlikely, as that would have been the equivalent of roughly US$50,000 at a time when the poverty threshold in China was US$1.25 per day. The lesser figure of 4,000 yuan seems more reasonable; however, that would still be a very large sum of money for early twenty-first-century rural China, where wages were around 50 cents per hour.

Whatever the amount, the couple built a small home with a store on its front end. They stocked it with day-to-day necessities and opened their little venture with high hopes that the business would be successful and provide for the entire family. But, in such a small village, filled with poor farmers, business did not thrive; in fact, it was quite dismal. All too soon the government wanted loan repayments, and the young couple didn't have the money. For some time, they were able to stall the government, but even after three years of trying to make a go of it, the business was a failure. Scared of the consequences that would befall him—jail—Pelsang panicked and fled over the mountains to India, telling Dolma to follow him when the girls were old enough.

Abandoned, Dolma tried to hold things together, constantly hopeful that business would turn around, but eventually she gave up hope, closed the home and store they had built, and returned to her father's farm. Having deserted the business, Dolma hoped the government would give up on the loan; however, that was not the case. Instead, the store and its contents were seized, and eventually Dolma was found at the family farm, where payment was once again demanded. She had nothing to give. Seizing the property and contents of the store nowhere near covered the loan, and Dolma was warned that she would still need to cover the remainder.

Like Pelsang, Dolma was terrified she'd be put in prison, and, out of desperation, left her girls in the care of her father and sister. She went to

Lhasa and found work as a day laborer on construction sites. When work ran out in Lhasa, she went to Shigatse, working on construction crews. For the next year, she hid from the government, working whatever job she could find. Occasionally, she returned home for brief visits, bringing clothes and shoes for her girls and a little money for her father. On one of these visits, the police came and arrested her. She was put in jail and interrogated repeatedly. She begged and pleaded with them to let her go so she could work and earn money to pay back the loan. "Please, please," she pleaded repeatedly, "if I work, I can repay you little by little. Don't take me away from my girls." Out of pity, the officers granted Dolma one more opportunity to make good on the loan. "Pay back the loan," they warned, "or you will be arrested and put in jail permanently." She could either pay the amount owed, face jail, or leave Tibet; those were her choices.

Consumed with fear and hopelessness and the belief that everyone would be better off without her, she began to contemplate suicide. She had no desire to join Pelsang in India, even though she felt it was her duty to do so. Her home was with her family in Tibet. Not only could she not conceive of leaving her father and siblings; her girls were far too young to make such a long and dangerous journey, and leaving them behind was not an option she wanted to contemplate. Without her husband to help, the entire situation seemed impossible. The meager income she was able to acquire through backbreaking labor was barely enough to provide for her girls, let alone pay back an extraordinary amount of money. Death appeared to be a natural solution to a seemingly unsolvable problem. Ultimately, she knew it was wrong to kill herself, as it would ensure an unfortunate rebirth, but still the thought of dying haunted her.

Stubborn by nature, Dolma continued to hide from the police while performing day-labor work and making secretive visits home. All seemed lost when the police began harassing her father for information regarding the whereabouts of his daughter and son-in-law. He loved his daughter, but he was fed up with Dolma's stubbornness and the unlikelihood of her ever earning enough money to pay off the loan. Being harassed by the police was the last straw. With loving sternness, Dolma's father chastised her behavior; she could not continue hiding and needed to think about how her problems affected her family. He tried repeatedly to counsel her on the futility of her actions, believing she should go to her husband in India. Instead, headstrong Dolma continued to work in Lhasa, struggling each day with fear and anxiety. Her father's admonishments rang true and played on a loop in her mind as she worked. She knew he was right; she could not continue hiding from her predicament. As much as it pained her to consider leaving her family, with a heavy heart Dolma began making a plan to go to India.

Through Pelsang's friends in India, Dolma was put in touch with someone in Lhasa, where she began the secretive task of locating a guide. Pelsang assured her that she and the girls could cross the mountains, leave trouble behind, and claim a better future. Few in her small village even thought of leaving Tibet; they were, like Dolma had once been, quite happy in their lives as farmers and too busy surviving from day to day to consider facing the difficulty of such an expensive and difficult journey.

The three-hour bus ride from Lhoka to Lhasa had by now become very familiar to Dolma. Though plagued with nauseating motion sickness, she made frequent visits to the capital to meet with links to prospective guides. When, finally, her luck turned, she met with a guide and a small group of Tibetans who were planning a crossing in the coming weeks.

The guide, three elderly women, and five young adults were completely unaware of her circumstances as they talked about the details of the trek. Fearing rejection, Dolma hid her plan to take her two girls with her. She also had one additional secret: she had no money to pay the guide. Dolma felt ashamed to be in a situation so desperate that she would lie to save herself and her children, but the circumstances forced dishonesty. She would wait until the last minute to uncover the details of her situation instead, and pray for mercy.

Returning to Lhoka to prepare her things and say goodbye to her family, she discovered her father had constructed a backpack for her and loaded it with tsampa and clothes for his granddaughters. Tearfully, he pressed the bag into his daughter's hands; it would be the last time he would see his youngest child. Dolma struggled to hold back tears as she said her farewells. Leaving her family was the most painful thing she'd ever had to do in her life, and the promise of reuniting with Pelsang provided little comfort. He had abandoned her and their children, and little by little Dolma's heart had grown cold and angry toward him. Now, as a result of his actions, she was left in an unwinnable situation.

As her father bent down to embrace his grandchildren, Dolma put the pack on her back, furiously swiping away her tears. Her elder sister held Dolma's face in her hands, pressed her forehead to her sister's, and whispered, "Happy, healthy, long life, little sister. I will pray for your safe journey."

Dolma choked out an instruction to take care of their father and be happy: "I will pray for you every day." For the last time, she crossed the threshold of her family home and, with her two little girls, stepped into the unknown.

When Dolma showed up at the designated meeting place in Lhasa with her five-and six-year-old daughters in tow, the group of strangers whom she had met only once before burst out with admonitions and questions. "What are you thinking? This is a very difficult journey! You cannot take babies. How can you do this?"

Dolma begged and pleaded, explaining her situation: "Please don't say no; I have no other choice."

The guide, Lobsang, was incredulous. "What are you thinking?! It will be very difficult for such small children. How can you do this? It is so far to walk with babies!"

"I have to; I can't stay here. My situation is very bad here; I have no other choice." Dolma quickly explained her situation: that her husband had left her to deal with the debt, that the police had threatened her with jail, and that she feared being taken away from her girls. Dolma's tears and pleading softened the barrage of negativity, and the room grew very quiet as everyone considered her plight. Lobsang eyed her silently. He had good reason to hesitate. He'd been over the mountains many times and knew exactly what was before them. Treacherous and deadly, the trek had taken the lives of people far stronger than Dolma. He could see she was strong-willed, though, and gradually softened as the group began to rally around Dolma. "We will all take turns carrying the girls."

"Yes, we can help her; it will work."

Then she dropped her second bomb: "I have no money to pay you, only 100 yuan."

Lobsang only snorted and shook his head. "Of course!"

"I will work when I get to Nepal and pay you then. Please, please!" Dolma assured him.

Lobsang had seen just about everything in his time as a guide to Tibetans wishing to cross the mountains to India, so this was no surprise; always someone was desperate and penniless; Dolma's financial revelations were an unpleasant truth that Lobsang had dealt with before. He continued to question her, sizing her up the entire time. For several long, quiet moments, he peered into her tear-streaked face and finally nodded his approval—though against his better judgment.

In short order, it was unanimously agreed everyone would alternate carrying the girls throughout the trek. After previously scolding Dolma, they got on with the business of solving the problem they now faced together: how to support this woman and her two children. Immediately, two of the younger adults set about dealing with practicalities like buying extra shoes and food for Dolma's girls. Providing for the well-being of two small children was of the highest concern. Relieved to have her secrets out in the open, and accepted, Dolma began to see a glimmer of hope in her future. If nothing else, she knew her girls would stand a better chance of crossing the mountains than she had originally believed.

Late that night, the group of twelve were in a truck headed west out of Lhasa to Mt. Kailash. Of all the sacred sites in Tibet, Kailash (*Kang Rinpoche,* in Tibetan, translated as "*Precious Jewel of Snows*"), located nearly 900 miles southwest of Lhasa, is top of the list. Religious pilgrims from Tibet, India, and Nepal frequent the holy mountain, so it made sense that the group might throw off any suspicion by posing as devout Buddhists. The sacred mountain is fewer than 100 miles from the Nepal border. From there, the trekkers would cover the remaining 250 miles on foot, winding through the mountains to Kathmandu.

Even among non-Tibetan Buddhists such as those of the Hindu, Jain, and Bön religions, the mountain is regarded as one of the holiest places on earth. Visiting the area—and circumambulating for 32 miles around the base of the mountain at an average altitude of 15,000 feet—is considered a great privilege. In some areas the path reaches 18,000 feet, and yet pilgrims remain undeterred in the task of prostrating and or walking the entire kora multiple times. Posing as pilgrims was no hardship for anyone in the group. Instead, visiting Mt. Kailash was viewed as an appropriate and auspicious opportunity to gain merit, erase bad karma, and bring good fortune to the journey ahead.

Like many guides, Lobsang promised a trek of, at most, four days to Kathmandu. He believed that telling people the truth would deter them from undertaking the passage—not good for business. In truth, the entire trip could take three weeks or more, depending on how fast the group could travel. With young children accompanying them, they would have to move more slowly than normal, and this reality nagged at Lobsang as they embarked on what would have been a dangerous journey under the best of circumstances.

After two days spent visiting the mountain, it was time to set out on the remainder of their long journey. The truck could not take them all the way to the border from Mt. Kailash; it would bring too much attention. Stopping at the southern tip of Lake Manasarovar, they camped for the night, sneaking away on foot before the early-morning light.

In a piece of strong cloth tied around her chest like a sling, Dolma carried her youngest girl, Yeshe, on her back. By her side, six-year-old Tseyang trudged along, holding tight to her mother's hand. Tseyang, like any six-year-old, often wanted to walk on her own. She moved along under the watchful eye of her mother or one of the elderly women. The girls didn't complain too much, though curious Tseyang had to be watched carefully else she would stray from the path. True to their word, the younger adults in the party took turns carrying the girls on their backs, especially when the terrain became too dangerous for young feet to navigate. The backpack Dolma's father had fashioned for her made the rounds as well, and Dolma's spirits lifted in appreciation of the generosity and compassion heaped upon her and the girls. Her fears slowly began to lift, and her cheerful resolve returned; she and her girls would make it to India.

Her girls were precious, and in no way did she ever consider her undertaking lightly. From her perspective, she quite simply had run out of options and had been forced to flee. She could scarcely believe she was actually in the midst of walking her children through the great mountains. Pelsang had told her that the girls would be safe in India and, unlike herself, would have access to an education through the network of Tibetan Children's Village (TCV) schools. As long as they made it safely across, their future would be better than hers, and with the passing of each day she resolved herself to that belief. Now, trudging through the mountains, she clung fervently to the hope that her children would be better off in India.

Even with help from the young adults in the group, Dolma fretted about her daughters. No one was eating enough food—that was clear—and Tseyang tugged at her mother's chuba several times a day: "Mama, I'm hungry."

"Soon, soon, my dear, we will stop and eat." Dolma knew full well that when they did finally stop, there would be little to eat, and certainly not enough to fill Tseyang's empty belly, or anyone else's. Even so, Dolma committed herself to a happy attitude, chirping encouragement to the girls and chatting animatedly with her companions.

More than two weeks into the trek, the food supply was finished; there was not a morsel of food left between the ten adults. The girls were exhausted, as was everyone else. Though no one spoke of it, Dolma knew the girls were slowing their progress. Early in the morning one day, Lobsang announced that he and the five younger Tibetans were splitting off and going a different way. Fear had gotten the better of them—maybe hunger and fatigue as well. They had grown increasingly paranoid about being arrested. As young Tibetan students, they would surely be thrown in jail and tortured, they claimed. They would leave the older women, Dolma, and the girls to reach Nepal's border on their own. Dolma was devastated. "No, no, you cannot leave us, we will never make it!" Without their help, how would she ever get her children safely to Nepal?

"We are sorry, sister; we must take a different route to avoid police. It will be too difficult for you. If we take the easy route with you, we will be caught."

"But what about us?"

"Three grandmothers and a young mother won't be suspected; they won't bother you."

Lobsang assured her that the border of Nepal was not far away, and that she and the older women could make it. He gave careful directions to the women, and then he and the others turned and walked away. They would never meet again.

Abandoned first by her husband and now by strangers she had trusted and relied upon, Dolma's resolve crumbled. It seemed that everywhere she turned, hardship and failure waited to greet her with punishing blows. Left behind while trekking across the most forbidding mountains in the world, she felt she'd been dealt the final setback, and it broke her. Forsaken in the wilds of the Snow Mountains with two small children, no food, and three women past their prime, Dolma succumbed to uncontrollable tears that refused to abate, even with the gentle urgings of the women and her young daughters. The girls' tiny shoes were now worn through and falling apart. As they talked with Dolma, the women tore strips of cloth from the hems of their skirts and tied the remains of the small shoes together. Like grandmothers, they offered gentle kindness to Dolma's precious little jewels.

Through her veil of tears, Dolma watched these women care for her girls while also attempting to cheer her with silly stories and jokes. Up to this point, she had refused to believe they would fail to reach India. Instead, she fought to push away her nagging fears that tragedy would befall her and her daughters, and instead focused on reuniting with Pelsang and a new life in India. She had let herself believe she was among people she could trust and rely on; she felt betrayed, just as she had when her husband had left her with debt and two children. The elder women repeatedly promised Dolma that they would not abandon her, that they would stay together to the very end and take care of each other, no matter what happened. There was nothing left to do but go on.

Slowly, the tired and hungry group made their way down the mountains. Dolma's tears receded and her willful nature, though slightly deflated, emerged once again. The girls, in their mended shoes, stumbled frequently, but their hands were always in the firm grasp of one or more women, and sometimes they were hoisted onto aging backs.

Coming upon a small village in the crest of a valley, two of the women posed as pilgrims and went begging for food. Not an uncommon practice in remote areas like this, villagers gave what they could. The small bags of tsampa, dried cheese, and tea would get them to the Nepalese border. After days of hunger, Dolma's girls gorged themselves till their little bellies were full, resulting in a bout of diarrhea for the remainder of the day, which the older women did not know to anticipate. Despite the girls needing to stop often, the women were fortified by food and continued to pick their way through the remaining valleys and mountains, after two days eventually reaching Nepal.

Dolma was lucky to be in the company of these elderly women; in both Tibetan and Nepali culture, elders are looked after with great care and respect. A kindly Nepali man took the women under his wing and ensured they reached the TRRC in Kathmandu. There, Dolma was relieved for the first time in many, many months. Not only had she and the girls made it safely across the mountains, but she was also now completely free from the pressure of the government debt and the threat of going to prison. She allowed herself to relax and enjoy a short respite.

At the refugee center, Dolma was introduced to indoor plumbing—a great novelty and a convenience that Dolma had never experienced, and for the first time in their lives, she and the girls took showers. She soaped, shampooed, and scrubbed her daughters till their skin and hair were free of any speck of dirt. Then she turned the same careful attention upon herself. New clothes and beds to sleep on seemed to her a luxury. But relief only lasted for a couple of days before a new pressure descended upon her: money.

Never one to sit idle, Dolma went in search of work. In fact, all she could think about was earning money, so much so that she left the refugee center without being properly processed, and obtained no refugee identification documents. It didn't even occur to her that such documentation would be important; she had no experience to counsel her otherwise. While other newcomers were taking classes to learn English or laying around, enjoying the warmth and allowing their bodies to heal from the grueling ordeal of walking across the Himalayas, Dolma went to work. She arranged for the girls to stay at the center under the care of the workers there, while she lived and worked in a restaurant owned by a friend of her husband. For the next six months, she earned 500 rupees a week (approximately US$7 at the time) and visited her daughters as often as she could. Dolma was happy that she and her girls were finally safe, and she was earning more money than she ever had performing day labor. Dolma worked and earned while Pelsang was finishing his schooling at the Tibetan Transit School (TTS) in Dharamsala.

In no hurry to reunite with his family, Pelsang took his time to collect his wife and daughters from Kathmandu. Eventually, he did arrive, and he took the girls and Dolma to Dehradun and the Tibetan settlement of Dekyiling. Always looking for a way to earn money, Dolma quickly found work at the Mindrolling Ladrang Monastery in Clement Town, also in Dehradun, working as household help. She happily and gratefully cooked and cleaned for an honored Rinpoche for three years. Pelsang worked as a delivery driver, and between the two of them they were financially comfortable for the first time in their lives.

Much to Dolma's dismay, the girls were enrolled in the TCV boarding school, also in Dehradun. She didn't want to be away from her daughters anymore, but between the Rinpoche and Pelsang insisting the girls needed an education to enrich their lives and ensure a successful future, she relented. Education was for her girls' benefit, even if it meant Dolma would not see them every day. Not wealthy or even middle class by any stretch, Pelsang and Dolma were merely comfortable and safe, and the girls were getting the education neither parent had ever had.

Dehradun has hosted the smaller Tibetan settlement of Dekyiling since 1981, and Pelsang and Dolma felt somewhat at home among Tibetan-speaking neighbors. They all shared a common plight, separated from their families in Tibet and living in a strange new land. India was peculiar and at times unfathomable, and the humid heat was nearly unbearable in the summer months, but Dolma and Pelsang no longer had the cloud of a debt they couldn't pay hanging over their heads. The girls were safe and were receiving a good education; their future would be better.

Working for a Rinpoche was an honor for Dolma. Not only was he an important figure in the Tibetan Buddhist tradition, but he was also kind and compassionate. Mindrolling Ladrung of the Nyingma tradition of Tibetan Buddhism has its roots in Tibet, as do all the Tibetan monasteries currently in India. In 1959, twenty-nine-year-old Trichen Jurme Kinzang Wangya was ready for enthronement as the Eleventh Mindrolling Trichen. The plans were thwarted by the ensuing chaos of the Tibetan uprising in Lhasa on March 10, 1959, and the full Chinese occupation of Tibet that followed. Leaving behind the Tibetan monastery originally established in 1676, Trichen fled into a life of exile in India. Three years later, in 1962, he was officially enthroned, but he was only able to establish a new monastery in 1976, choosing Dehradun as its home. Mindrolling has since flourished into one of the largest Buddhist centers in the world, and one of the most beautiful in India.

Often, Dolma's Rinpoche employer encouraged her to go to Dharamsala to see His Holiness the Fourteenth Dalai Lama. It was an opportunity she should not miss for any reason, he told her. While living in Lhasa, Dolma had repeatedly heard the name Kundun spoken with great reverence by Tibetans. She had known he had left Tibet many years before and that his absence was a heartache for many Tibetans. She had seen small pictures of him from time to time that pilgrims concealed deep in the folds of their chubas—China considers his image an illegal possession—and she had understood that even speaking his name out loud in public could incur swift retribution from the PRC. However, Dolma thought of the Dalai Lama as just another revered Rinpoche from Tibet's past, like one of the many statues in every monastery she'd ever been in. When in Lhasa, she had seen people bowing before ornate golden statues in the Jokhang Temple and assumed that one of them had to be the Dalai Lama. The same was true at Mindrolling; after prostrating in front of statues, devotees would place offerings around the beautiful golden depictions of holy Rinpoches of the past. Did she really need to leave work and travel all the way to Dharamsala to see a statue? But at the Rinpoche's insistence, she relented. The Rinpoche made the arrangements for her visit, which was to coincide with that of another group of pilgrims, and off to Dharamsala she went.

In a small room at the Tsuglagkhang Temple, Dolma sat among a small group of Tibetans gathered expectantly for an audience with the Dalai

Lama. Scanning the room, she was slightly confused. Why were they sitting together in this room? Shouldn't they be in the temple, lined up to prostrate at the great statue of the Dalai Lama? Would they carry the statue into the room? How big would it be? Would it be gold, or bronze studded with jewels, or turquoise, jade, or pearls, like so many of the statues of great Lamas she had seen in so many temples? Believing that the Dalai Lama was not a living being but a god that the faithful prayed to, Dolma patiently waited for the great statue to arrive. Soon, a retinue of monks in maroon robes shuffled into the room, accompanied by burly crew-cut Tibetan men in Western suits. When a small, cheerful man in red robes took his place in the ornate chair on the center dais and began talking to the group of Tibetans, Dolma was astounded. He wasn't a statue; here was the man she had seen in pictures; the Dalai Lama was alive! So overwhelmed at the shock of this realization, Dolma fainted into a heap among her fellow Tibetans. Immediately, the Dalai Lama popped up from his seat and moved to Dolma's slumped figure. Hovering with great concern, he blew on her face and fanned at her with his hands. He continued touching her face and head to make sure she was still breathing, then instructed his aides to carry Dolma to the front, near his seat, so he could keep an eye on her.

Slowly, Dolma regained consciousness; still confused and incredulous, she could only stare at the flesh-and-blood man so often referred to as a god. *How could he be real?* she wondered. He smiled and chuckled at her from his seat, waggled his index finger at her, then continued his informal speech. As he often does, the Dalai Lama directed his advice toward maintaining a positive attitude, regardless of the adversity encountered in one's life. "Be happy; now you are in a free country, you are safe, so no more need to worry." He assured the attentive group that he would pray for all of them.

Following his talk, the devotees lined up to offer the ceremonial khata to His Holiness, as is the tradition. Knees quaking violently, Dolma stumbled forward to offer the white silken scarf to this flesh-and-blood human. Bowing so deeply in front of the Dalai Lama that her forehead almost touched his knees, she could barely breathe. Tears ran in uncontrollable rivulets down her face; deep emotion enveloped her entire being as the Dalai Lama took the khata from her hands and placed it around her neck.

Reaching down, he gently grasped her elbows, pulling her upright enough to put his forehead against hers for a moment. The world melted away; Dolma could hear only his voice, see only his bare arms and red robes. She momentarily lost the power to speak or move. "I will pray for you. Calm down; everything will be good now. There is no need to worry." He spoke in a soothing tone that slowed Dolma's breathing. He then took her hand and pressed his picture into her palm. Very suddenly, her mind was crystal-clear, unlike anytime she had known in the past. As she was led away, she nearly burst out laughing as joy spread through her mind and body like a cool fire. Suffering and hardship seemed so very far away now, life so simple and uncomplicated; there truly was nothing to fear.

Meeting the Dalai Lama had lifted Dolma's spirits to soaring heights that, unfortunately, she could not maintain for long. Generally, she exercised a positive outlook on life, one that could come crashing down if she was pushed too far, as had happened in Tibet and while crossing the mountains. The years to follow her jubilant meeting with the Dalai Lama would bring heartache and difficulty that would challenge the most optimistic of people.

Restless and ever the dreamer, Pelsang wanted to work for himself, and set about convincing Dolma to start another business. With its large Western tourist trade, Goa, India was the place to be. As fortune would have it, Pelsang had a lead on a friend selling his jewelry business before emigrating to America. Borrowing 50,000 rupees from the Rinpoche and an additional 200,000 from a monastery in Delhi, the couple supplied themselves with jewelry and goods to make their own malas and necklaces of semi-precious stones, turquoise, coral, amber, and amethyst. Taking over the roadside stall, where tourists provided a brisk business, Dolma and Pelsang embarked on their second attempt at running a business, working seven days a week from morning until after dark most days. The Goa jewelry trade proved profitable enough that the loans were paid back in a short amount of time, and finally the two had a successful business.

But Pelsang began to change. Alcohol became a dominant presence in his daily routine and sometimes he would lash out at Dolma and physically assault her. When the girls returned home from school for visits, they begged their mother not to stay with Pelsang for fear he would kill her. The assaults worsened, and finally Dolma realized she could no longer endure this treatment from her husband. Her girls were correct: Pelsang was getting worse, growing increasingly violent, neglecting the business and leaving Dolma to work the stall all day. After all he had put her through over the years, she'd finally had enough. Taking a portion of the jewelry supplies and money, she moved to a different section of the city and set up her own simple stall. It was there that she met Kunchok.

Kunchok's jewelry stall was not far from Dolma's, and being the convivial sort, he was friendly with all his neighbors. Passing the time chatting, sharing tea, or helping others, everyone within a block or two knew Kunchok. It wasn't long before Dolma captured his attention. Kunchok had also experienced problems with his former wife and, though nearly penniless, like Dolma he too was beginning his life anew. The two bonded over their shared experience and misfortune, and the rest, as they say, is history. By their own admission, Dolma and Kunchok were like two beggars coming together to start life over.

Eventually the heat and humidity of Goa became too much for Dolma, and the couple moved to McLeodganj, where the temperatures were cooler throughout the year. She had grown accustomed to the girls being in boarding school and seeing them only during holidays, and realized she needed to live where the climate suited her health better. With a strong tourist trade, business in McLeodganj was brisk and they continued to prosper enough to make ends meet—and save a little money, too.

Kunchok was a good husband to Dolma, and he loved Yeshe and Tseyang too. But he longed for his own child—a boy was his dream—and it weighed heavily on Kunchok. Little by little, he convinced Dolma to have another baby; in 2014, to Kunchok's delight, his strong and lovely wife gave birth to a boy. Just one, she had told him: "No more children now; I am done."

Dolma was seven months pregnant with Kunchok's baby when first we met. We connected almost immediately, though we had very little shared language. Our friendship grew into a sisterhood. I visited her often, watching her string beads for malas, amazed at how deft she was at this task. Sometimes, I would help her design jewelry, laying out beads in patterns that she would then adjust and turn into necklaces, earrings, and bracelets. The three of us shared many meals together at my home and theirs, with Kunchok acting as translator and always offering to clean up afterwards. He was kind and attentive to both of us and was looking forward to being a father for the first time.

Dolma had a difficult delivery and, halfway through her labor, was sent to another hospital, a forty-five-minute taxi ride away. When Kunchok told me the story a couple of days later, I was horrified at what she must have gone through. In the end, Dolma gave birth to a baby boy, her last child, and Kunchok was ecstatic to have a son—though I was baffled when he told me they would send the boy to a monastery when he turned three or four years old. Kunchok was hoping his son would turn out to be the reincarnation of a great Rinpoche. I understand this is a common practice in Tibetan families, and considered an honor, but all I could think about was how much Dolma had suffered to bring this baby into the world, only to have him given away to a monastery.

Many times in the weeks prior to the baby's birth, I had offered the use of my shower to Dolma. Knowing they didn't have one, I thought she would appreciate a good scrub all over. Finally, a few weeks after the baby was born, she took me up on the offer to use my shower. Unbeknownst to me, it had been a year since she had last had a full shower. After a half-hour or so, she emerged from the bathroom, coaxing me to come in and look. I wasn't sure what the problem was. Thinking she had run into an issue with the drain or shower, I stuck my head in at the doorway and saw clumps of tan all over the floor. Her skin had shed like a snake after so many months of not bathing, leaving little piles of dead skin. Admittedly, I was very grossed-out. We had a good laugh, though; we agreed it was icky, and made faces at each other, and noises in lieu of language. Ever diligent, she set about cleaning the floor until it was spotless.

Disposable diapers were a novelty to Dolma. When I brought a pack to her with other gifts for the baby, she didn't quite know what to do with them. Thus far, she had been wrapping the baby in thin blankets that she would wash when soiled. I showed her how the diapers worked and the next day, and many thereafter, found them hanging from clothespins after having been washed. I elected to stay silent on that front, since there was no harm in her washing and reusing the diapers as long as they held up.

With Losar—the Tibetan New Year—just a few weeks away, Dolma insisted that we shop for fabric to make new chubas to wear for the celebrations. She and Kunchok were intent on me celebrating the Tibetan New Year with them, and this required appropriate attire. I was not keen on wearing the traditional clothing of a culture not my own, as it felt like an offensive appropriation, but Dolma insisted.[1] Early one morning we met outside the couple's tiny room, and I helped her strap the baby to her back in a cloth sling, and off we went. The walk is all downhill, for about twenty minutes. Dolma and I chatted in our odd way of communicating, with the few words we both knew in each other's language—hand signs, facial expressions, and miming. Dolma was an expert haggler and made sure we got a good price for the cloth we wanted, and then we were off to the tailor, where she once again negotiated the price. She also let it be known that my hiking boots were not to be worn with my new chuba. There is a great deal of social pressure in Tibetan culture, and I was pulled into the expectation that I wear the correct clothing and look properly Tibetan for the celebrations.

After spending the better part of the day walking to and from the Tsuglagkhang complex, partaking in the rituals, prostrating at the appropriate times, turning many prayer wheels, repeatedly tossing tsampa pinched between my thumb and forefinger into the air, and being introduced to many

Tibetan women whom I believe Dolma was trying to impress, we headed home for food and libations. Kunchok had prepared a huge bowl of what he referred to as "buff," which I believe was either water buffalo meat or beef from cows, the latter of which would have been extremely dangerous to have procured, as cows are considered sacred in India. Either way, given it was sitting out when I arrived early that morning and it was now early evening, I elected not to partake. When the day's activities ended, and visitors departed, Kunchok switched on the television to watch Tibet TV broadcasted from Lhasa.[2] We watched Tibetans in beautiful brocade-and-silk chubas dancing to traditional Tibetan music and singing on elaborate stage sets. All the Tibetans appeared happy, and yet I felt something false in all the performances: forced and sanitized compared to the performances I'd seen so many times in Dharamsala, where the emotion that emanated from the performers felt genuine. The smiles of the TV performers seemed frozen in place, never faltered, never fluctuated—well-rehearsed, pretending to be happy.

Sitting quietly next to me, Dolma began to weep. Tears trickled down her face and she began to explain her feelings as I put my arm around her and drew her close. Kunchok explained that she was homesick, missed her family in Tibet, and was sad that she couldn't be there to celebrate the new year with them, in her homeland. After six years, she still longed for her home and family. This was the first time I had seen Dolma anything other than smiling and happy, and I wasn't the least bit surprised.

Nearly ten years later, I had lost track of both Kunchok and Dolma. Our main form of connection had been via WeChat, a Chinese app much like WhatsApp. When I finally managed to track Kunchok down through a mutual acquaintance, I was shocked to discover he was in Paris. Where was Dolma? Was he bringing her to Paris? How had he gotten there? He responded with Dolma's WhatsApp contact info and nothing else. Knowing she couldn't speak, read, or write in English, I relied on the same friend to send a message to her. She was still in McLeodganj, her son was in a monastery, her daughters were finishing college in southern India, and she was living in a small, dank room, barely getting by. She was ill and very unhappy. Kunchok had left Dolma for a Tibetan woman in Paris who could get him out of India. Dolma was abandoned and broken-hearted yet again. When we finally were able to connect via a WhatsApp call, my friend translated while Dolma and I cried at her misfortune. Her health had taken a turn, and she had kidney stones. I immediately sent her money and asked her to find a better place to live, a room with sun, a proper bathroom with a shower and hot water. We counseled her to eat lots of fruit and vegetables, to maintain a better diet, and to continue seeking medical help. There was nothing I could say to heal her broken heart.

As of this writing, Dolma is healthier, happier, and has a large room with enough space to accommodate her daughters when they visit. She can also afford to visit her son at his monastery whenever she wants. She continues to sell jewelry in McLeodganj, and we maintain regular contact. It is highly unlikely that Dolma will ever leave India. Her past offense with the Chinese government will not have been forgotten, even after so many years. This prevents her from going home, whether through legal channels or not. Her children are all in India as well, and they too are unlikely to leave a nation that has become their home.

CHAPTER 3

SISTERS

Not all Tibetan nuns shave their heads. Ani B has long, fine-textured, dark hair coiled into a bun on the top of her head. She has a face that radiates kindness and clarity, and gentleness beams through a smile that puts others at ease. Her slender frame is swathed in the traditional colors of the Tibetan Buddhist faith; her hats, coats, socks, shirts, skirts, and shawls are all reddish-maroon of varying hues. Ani B may dress monochromatically, but her personality is far from one-dimensional. In fact, she is a delight to be around. Typically jovial, affectionate, and chatty, she makes her declarations of love to her friends with comedic abandon, declaring in the few English words she knows, "I loooove yoooou," drawing out the words in a singsong pattern. When she speaks in Tibetan her words are a blur, punctuated with exclamations, saliva slurps, and often interspersed with hearty giggles. Switching to English slows her down as she searches for words and the correct pronunciation. "My English very bad!" Self-deprecation is Ani B's forte, as much as complimenting and finding the best in others. "You are very kind; you are very good"—always she says this with sincere appreciation lightened by joviality; humor is as prominent a force in her life as her religious dedication. Though she may sound like she's kidding, she truly means every word.

Long before sunrise, Ani B would wake and read scriptures. In a quiet monotone mumble she would read from the long slender pieces of block-print—loose-leaf Buddhist scripture books. An hour each morning was devoted to scripture before breakfast, and then she would walk the five-mile kora circuit around the Tsuklakhang complex in McLeodganj. The remainder of her day usually involved some combination of English-language study, more Buddhist study, cooking, cleaning, laundry, food shopping, visiting with friends, and, of course, chatting with an assortment of friends and family via the Chinese app WeChat.

Ani B chose to live independently, rather than ensconced in a nunnery. She liked her freedom, and though she had taken up residence for some time in a nunnery after reaching India, she'd ended up choosing independence for reasons that were her own. Living alone did not mean she was lonely, though; she gathered regularly with other nuns for meals and camaraderie and had developed many lay friends in the small community.

Her life in India was like everyone else's around her: uncertain. Would she live out her days in the mountains of Dharamsala, watching the steady stream of Tibetan newcomers arrive, while others she had become close to departed to faraway places? Would she go back to Tibet and live with her younger sister? Or would she be one of the lucky few who somehow went abroad? She tried to keep these thoughts in the back of her mind while going through the motions of each day.

Ani B had made her way to India to be among the many high Rinpoches of Tibetan Buddhism, with the Karmapa being the most important to her, as a member of the Kagyu sect of the religion that she studied. She knew she could study freely in India, without fear of reprisal or interference from the Chinese government. Like most monastics, she received a small stipend from her order to provide the basics needed to survive. Her meager funds helped pay for her tiny room and necessities.

At a young age, Ani B knew this would be her life: religion and study, no husband, no children. A life devoted to her Buddhist faith. Stories of all the holy places of Nepal and India had reached her ears even in childhood, fueling a desire to see the great shrines and holy places of the Buddha. When she became a nun in her late teens, her desire was kindled to a bright flame.

When Ani B's mother died at a fairly young age, her father and grandmother were left to raise Ani B and her younger sister, Yeshe. Ani B helped as much as possible, especially with the care of Yeshe. By the time she became a teen, she knew that leaving home for India was in her future. However, getting her father to agree to this would not prove easy. He had come to rely on her and, though he appreciated her religious devotion, he did not think being a nun was the best use of his eldest daughter's life. Thinking she would outgrow her obsession, he left it to time to change her ways. When she began to express her desire to go to India, she was met with great resistance. Both her father and grandmother forbade her to even think of it. Such a dangerous endeavor was not to be considered by a young woman on her own—nun or not.

For two years, Ani B continued to toy with the idea of mythical India and its holy places. Knowing her father would not approve, she suggested that instead of going to India, she should undertake a pilgrimage to Lhasa and Mt. Kailash instead. This idea was hard for her father to deny, since Tibetans wholeheartedly believe in pilgrimages to holy places, Lhasa and Kailash being two of the most important destinations. Still, her father was not completely convinced and continued to generally resist her persistence on the topic.

When she confided to seventeen-year-old Yeshe that despite her father's objections she planned to go on pilgrimage, her little sister begged to accompany her. In their mother's absence, Ani B had become Yeshe's substitute mother, and the two were nearly inseparable. The thought of being parted was unthinkable, especially for Yeshe. At the time, Ani B did not disclose her plans for India, but began to ponder whether her younger sister should accompany her on that part of the journey as well. A pilgrimage was one thing, but to take her across the mountains, abandoning their father and grandmother completely and putting her sister's life at risk, was something altogether different.

Like many traditional Nomadic families, Ani B's had camped with the grazing animals in high pastures during the warm summer months. After many weeks living in the hills and tending to the animals, she decided it was time to begin her pilgrimage. Come fall, the family would decamp from the mountains and retire to a small, rammed-earth home to survive winter on the harsh plateau. Against her father's wishes, she hatched her plan. Creative and cunning, as many with strong desires are, the two sisters would sneak away from the high-mountain encampment late at night, while everyone was sleeping. Waiting till the moon was full, late one night, Ani B gently woke her sister and told her it was time to leave. Well-versed in the terrain, the sisters easily picked their way down the mountain with the light of the stars and moon to guide them to the family's winter home. Ani B picked the lock on the only door of the small earthen home, and the girls snuck in and took a few yuan, some clothes, and a little tsampa and dried cheese. Without a map or directions to follow, the two headed out in what Ani B thought the most likely bearing toward Lhasa. Their pilgrimage had begun.

The plateau is vast, wild, and largely uninhabited, and its immense presence left Ani B feeling exposed and vulnerable in a way she had never felt when surrounded by family. She was frightened—so much so that at times she felt like she was outside of her body, ungrounded by the fear that took hold of her. The idea of wild animals, hungry ghosts, or any number of unknown terrifying fates awaiting her and Yeshe invaded her thoughts throughout the first week of the trek. They were truly alone in the untamed wilderness; however, in reality, there was little to fear except for the raging rivers that continually crisscrossed their path. Rivers and tributaries of varying sizes snake out across the plateau like highways on a map; rushing down from the Himalayas, the "Water Tower of Asia," they carve long, deep, icy grooves. Yeshe and Ani B crossed many of these powerful and frigid waters during the initial weeks of their journey. Although neither could swim, they were not strangers to river crossings; yet it was almost always a death-defying undertaking. To avoid any mishaps, sometimes the sisters would walk for miles along a stretch, hoping to find a break in the swift current or a shallow area. Other times, they had to hold tight and pull each other through the rapidly moving frigid waters. During one such endeavor, a man happened along as they were about to enter the river. He jumped in the water and helped them safely across, then returned and went on his way, as if he had just escorted two damsels in distress across a busy highway.

Figuring that her father would send someone to come looking for his errant daughters, Ani B wanted to stay away from roads, where they might be detected. She was determined to see this pilgrimage through, no matter what, and even in the grip of nearly paralyzing fear in the early days, she stayed stubbornly true to her goal. The river crossings, however, worried her younger sister a great deal.

"Maybe we can't go to Lhasa if we have so many rivers to cross, and still there are more, always another and another."

Taking her younger sister's hand and smiling at her innocence, Ani B consoled her. "Yes, my dear, there are many rivers and there will be many more to come, but we have taken a decision, so now we must continue. Don't be discouraged, sister, only think of our destination; we are going to Lhasa!" From then on, Yeshe didn't utter a single complaint. Whether she held them inside or abandoned them Ani B did not know, but she was proud of her younger sibling's power to adapt to difficulty.

For an entire month they walked, crossing rivers, sleeping on the hard ground, begging for food from nomads and other travelers they met along the way, and befriending many pilgrims headed for various holy destinations throughout Tibet. It was the pilgrims they encountered along the journey who helped the sisters continue. They shared similar goals and values, and a generosity of spirit increased by the challenges of a holy pursuit. Many pilgrims simply walk to their destination, murmuring prayers as they finger their mala beads. Others stretch the length of their bodies along the ground, rise up, take two steps, and prostrate again; repeatedly performing this act represents the intensity of their religious devotion. Regardless of how they get there, for Tibetans, a pilgrimage to sacred sites, ancient mountains, monasteries, and ruins across unforgiving lands to pray is a chance to gain merit, wash away the karma of the past, and bring good fortune and blessings to one's current life, ensuring a positive rebirth in the next.

As they journeyed together, Ani B grew fond of each of these strangers. At night, the band of pilgrims would make a fire and gather around its light and warmth to share stories of the past, the gods and high Rinpoches, the day-to-day gossip of their lives, and their hopes for the future. In these moments, Ani B's humor shone brightly as she joked and told funny stories. She felt safe and relaxed among kindred spirits.

For the final leg of the journey to Lhasa, Ani B, Yeshe, and some of the pilgrims they had befriended accepted a ride in the back of a lorry. The big truck grumbled and bounced its way into the city. "The Potala, the Potala!" one man exclaimed, pointing toward the huge white building high on a hilltop in the distance. Never had Ani B even seen a picture of the Potala, and she was unsure of what he was pointing at or what to look for; then, up on a hill above the city, she saw the most amazing vision. She gazed at the building, with its many layers of whitewashed walls gleaming in the high-altitude sun, ecstatic that she had reached one of her most cherished goals, the holy city of Lhasa. As they wandered through the streets of the capital, Ani B felt a sense of pure overwhelm. The sisters had never seen a city, and their mouths gaped in wonder. So much to look at, so many people in one place, so much noise and bustle—she could barely process it all and lost all sense of direction, until she remembered to look at the sun to tell her which way was west and which was north. After wandering in the city for a few hours, they made their way to the Kyi Chu River outside Lhasa. When they came to a grove of willow trees by the water, they made camp, along with other pilgrims already settled down for the night.

Early the next morning, Ani B and Yeshe, along with several of the pilgrims they had befriended, made their way to the Jokhang Temple in the old quarter of Lhasa. Ani B cried tears of pure joy at the sight of the sacred statue of Jowo Shakyamuni. The sisters prostrated in front of the temple, along with several other people, where the biting wind and cold stung their eyes. "Are you crying, sister," Ani B joked to Yeshe, "or is it the wind?" The two giggled uncontrollably, emotions so stirred by having reached one of the holiest places in Tibet after such a long and grueling expedition.

The Barkhor Square, another important area the girls were eager to visit, spans a six-acre site and is home to the sacred Jokhang Temple, built initially by King Songsten Gampo. Lore has it that the king established the temple for his Chinese wife Wencheng and his Nepalese wife Brikhuti, both devout Buddhists. It was Princess Wencheng of the Tang Dynasty who brought the now-revered Jowo Shakyamuni statue to Tibet when she married King Songsten in the sixth century. The statue, as legend has it, was sculpted during the lifetime of—and blessed by—the Buddha, Siddhartha Gautama. Tibetans believe the icon is an emanation of the Buddha and has the power to transform negative energy, liberating one from disturbances of all kinds.

Neither of the sisters considered the historic underpinnings of the Jokhang; they only knew it was religiously significant to Tibetans and that to prostrate in front of the seventh-century temple would bring great merit. That both the Jokhang Temple and Jowo Shakyamuni survived the March 10 uprising and Mao's Cultural Revolution is nothing short of miraculous. During the fighting between Tibetans and the PLA in March of 1950, some of the Khampa tribesmen and others from Lhasa holed up in the Jokhang as a main point of resistance against the Chinese. Sixteen years later, during China's Cultural Revolution, the temple endured minor damage after being attacked by the Red Guard, but was eventually fully repaired by the mid-1980s. Interestingly, near one entrance to the temple stands an obelisk erected in 823 CE; 18 feet tall and slender, it is a dual-language peace treaty between the forty-first Tibetan king, Ralpacan, and Chinese Emperor Muzong of the Tang Dynasty. In direct contradiction of the Chinese Communist Party's claims that Tibet has always been part of China, the treaty reads in part:

> *Tibet and China shall abide by the frontiers of which they are now in occupation. All to the east is the country of Great China; and all to the west is, without question, the country of Great Tibet. Henceforth on neither side shall there be waging of war nor seizing of territory. If any person incurs suspicion, he shall be arrested; his business shall be inquired into, and he shall be escorted back.*

Apparently, peace treaties between nations come and go, regardless of carved stone's ability to endure the ages. But Ani B didn't notice this piece of Tibetan history before getting down to the business of prayer. In reverence and gratitude for her current great fortune, and feeling lucky to be alive and in Lhasa, the most important city in all of Tibet, alongside many other Tibetans, she and Yeshe prayed and repeatedly prostrated the full length of their bodies in front of the Jokhang for the better part of the day.

As usual, Ani B was joking with her sister, delighted to see her laugh after such a grueling trek from their home. The giggling girls drew the attention of a group of three monks, a nun, and a layman who happened to be from near their home in Namchung. Striking up a conversation, Ani B learned they were heading to Mt. Kailash in a few days. Her eyes grew wide in excitement: "Oh, we want to see Mt. Kailash too!" Ani B took a liking to them immediately. "Please, wherever you go, may we go with you? I feel safe with you, and I have my sister to protect too."

"I'm sorry, sister, there is only one truck going and it is already full," replied Penpa, the eldest monk in the group.

Determined as ever, Ani B pled, "Oh, please, brother, we have no money, but we will do what we can to help. Please ask if we can come too."

Ani B is charming, and when she shines her beam of joy on an unsuspecting person, it's nearly impossible to say no. It took very little to prod the elder monk into talking with the truck driver on her behalf. Penpa was unable to make headway with the driver, who could not be convinced that two small women would be no trouble. After failing, Penpa encouraged Ani B to go and talk to the driver herself. The driver had no idea what he was up against. Ani B begged, pleaded, and wrung her hands, plying her sincere charm toward the driver, who finally relented. Ani B and Yeshe would join the other forty pilgrims headed to Mt. Kailash in his truck. Successful in her endeavor, Ani B's eyes met Penpa's with a twinkling knowing. Just as she had convinced him, he had known she would convince the driver with her sweet charm too.

After several days squished in the back of a truck, being jostled along bad roads, Ani B sometimes doubted her choice. Occasionally, the roads were covered in snow and so dangerous that the pilgrims hollered for the driver to stop or slow down. To fight the discomfort and boredom, they passed the time with songs and stories, snacking and sleeping. When Yeshe was sleeping, Ani B confided in Penpa her wish to go to India. He nodded his head but said little more that "Mmm" and "Ah."

Walking the 750 miles to Mt. Kailash from Lhasa would have taken the sisters roughly three to four weeks. Regardless of how uncomfortable the truck was, they arrived at their destination much quicker than walking. As she climbed out of the truck bed, Ani B nearly broke into tears at the site of the rocky snow-covered mountain jutting up from the earth. So important was this mountain in her mind that she could barely believe her good fortune in reaching it. The pilgrims hastily made camp, prepared food, and ate dinner, stopping occasionally during their chores to gaze at the mountain. As night descended, the mountain became a shadow in the gloom, and Ani B finally tore her gaze away and closed her eyes to sleep. Over the next fourteen days, the band of pilgrim friends rose daily at three a.m. and began the fifteen-hour circumambulation of the mountain.[1] After several days, already weak from the long journey from her home, irregular meals of varying sustenance, and lack of deep sleep and proper rest, Ani B began to trudge wearily around the mountain. She was exhausted but refused to give up this crucial opportunity. Convinced her dedication and efforts would bring her good fortune in life, and erase her past sins from previous lifetimes as well as this one, by sheer will she rose each morning, bone-weary, and walked up and down and around the base of the enormous mountain. It might be the only opportunity she would ever have in her life to change her karma, and she would not give in to her bodily needs.

During kora around the mountain one day, a cousin from their village spotted the sisters. "Ho, ho, Ani B-la, Yeshe-la!" The girls were surprised to see someone they knew from so far away.

Smiling happily, Ani B greeted her relative: "Tashi Delek, brother, cherung deypo yin bey?"

He replied, "I am well sister, and how are the two of you?" After exchanging a few brief details about his journey and the girl's activities since they'd left home, their cousin Ringzin grew quiet. "I have a message from your grandmother."

Ani B and Yeshe looked at each other with a sense of dread. They'd probably broken their poor grandma's heart to pieces by running off in the middle of the night. Guilt washed over both girls. Ani B knew that what she had done was selfish, especially in taking her sister with her. But she'd felt such a strong need to embark on this journey that she could barely make sense of it. The reality of what she had done and the possibility that she would never see her grandmother or father again clenched at her heart.

With a sense of import, Ringzin said, "Your grandmother asked me to tell you to come home. 'Bring them back to me,' she said."

Ashamed and sad for their grandmother, Ani B reached for her sister's hand. Yeshe was the first to speak. "What should we do, sister?" She was deeply affected by this news, and uncertainty mixed with guilt creased her brow; as always, she looked to her older sister for guidance. Ani B didn't have an immediate answer.

"I don't know, Yeshe. We will see what happens."

All along, Ani B had been fretting over whether to bring her sister to India. It had weighed heavily on her mind. Now she understood that Yeshe should return home. She must take care of their grandmother, who was old and would not live much longer.

Hand in hand, the sisters walked back to their tent to settle in for the night. Ani B wondered how to tell her sister that she wouldn't return home with her. Just two days prior, an old nun from Lhasa had confided in Ani B that Penpa was going to India and might take her with him if she asked. When she had approached him, Penpa had told her that he wouldn't take anyone else with him, as he did not want to be responsible if someone died along the way. True to form, Ani B worked her magic. "If I die, then it is my responsibility, not yours. I am willing to take the chance—that is how badly I want to go to India."

Mystifeid but serious, Penpa had replied: "I don't know what will happen along the way. It is very dangerous, so do not blame me if something bad comes to you."

Earnestly, Ani B assured him, "Even if I die, it is okay; you can leave my body to the vultures and go. I will not blame you, I will have no regrets."

Shaking his head, the old monk replied, "I am old and have met many people, but no one quite like you. How can you say this, that you would sacrifice your life to go to India?" He half-smiled and chuckled. "Rei, rei, you can go… but your sister cannot come, under any circumstances. No argument!"

There was no question now; Yeshe and Ani B would part ways, not knowing if they would see each other again. How would she break the news to her sweet little sister? A few more days passed and still Ani B could not find the words or the timing to tell Yeshe the truth. Instead, she remained jovial and worked hard to make her sister laugh and forget her worries over their grandmother.

On the thirteenth day of circumambulating Mt. Kailash, Penpa approached Ani B. "Tomorrow night we leave for India." Her stomach dropped at the news. She still hadn't said a word to Yeshe, hadn't warned her or even hinted at her plan. "Are you ready?" he asked.

"No," she replied. With a heavy heart, she turned away and went in search of her cousin. The feeling of leaving her sister behind, never knowing when or if they would meet again, was far more difficult than she had ever imagined.

In the dark, Ani B ran back to the tent where Yeshe, Ringzin, and other relatives were gathered for an evening meal. She took Ringzin aside and confided that she was leaving for India but couldn't take her sister. "What should I do?" she pleaded, as if he would make the decision for her and erase her dilemma.

After a long pause, Ringzin replied reassuringly. "Don't worry; I will take care of your sister. If you've already decided, then don't worry about Yeshe. I will take care of her. Now you must go and tell Yeshe. Be brave, Ani B-la."

Ani B couldn't find the courage to look Yeshe in the eye and speak of her plan to go to India without her, so she circled her arms around her baby sister, drawing her as close as possible, and whispered in ear. "I am going to India with Penpa and the others tomorrow. You must go home and take care of our elders. They need you."

Yeshe recoiled instantly, trying to pull away from her sister's embrace. "What are you saying? No, sister, you can't leave me!"

Ani B held Yeshe tighter and continued whispering in her sister's ear. "I must go, dear, our lives have a different path. I am already a nun, and my path is different from yours. You have a chance to have a family someday and our father and grandmother both need you. You must go home. Grandmother is very upset about us now. If we leave like this, it will be very bad karma for us, and she will be heartbroken."

Yeshe began sobbing, and in a strangled cry whimpered, "How can you leave me?"

Looking into her sister's face and wiping at her tears, Ani B whispered gently, "In India life would be very hard for you, dear; for me, I can live in a nunnery. Life won't be so hard."

Yeshe, incredulous at her sister's revelation, continued to resist the news, repeatedly peppering her sister with the same questions. Ani B tried her best to soothe and assure her little sister that everything would be okay. Defiantly, Yeshe continued to plead, "I can cut my hair too; I can be a nun too. Please, sister."

Shaking her head, Ani B took a firm stance. "No, no, this is not for you; you have not chosen the life of a nun. I am a nun, and I can't change. You can go back and take care of the family. We will try later, after grandmother dies, and then you can be a nun if you want. I will see how things are in India and if it's okay, then we will see." Yeshe was silenced by the shock of what was happening. Ani B gently instructed her sister, "Grandmother is already old and won't be here for long. You listen to her and help her. Whatever you do, don't get married right away—or we cannot meet again. After grandma dies, if you still want to be a nun, then we can do that. And you can come to India, and we can stay together then."

The sobering reality slowly crept across Yeshe's face that her elder sister's mind was made up, and with nothing left to argue, she relented. Knowing she should be happy for her sister, who had the chance to reach a long-held goal, she put on a brave face. "Okay, I will do what you say. It's a good chance for you in India, so go, and I will go back to take care of grandmother. Everything will be fine. Don't worry about us. You have very good company for your journey."

Ani B hoped that once she reached India, everything would fall into place—that someday she would go back to Tibet and bring her sister to India, making their parting temporary.

Well past midnight, Yeshe silently helped her older sister pack her bag. "You go to sleep now, my dear sister. It is late and I will leave soon." Ani B lovingly fussed over her little sister as she said this, making sure she was as comfortable as possible on the floor. Smoothing her hair and memorizing Yeshe's face, she leant down and kissed her goodbye. As Ani B rose to make her way to the opening of the tent, Yeshe scrambled up from the floor and embraced her sister tightly. Both girls began to weep loudly, and could not let go of each other. Ringzin tried to pull them apart, but they were clinging to one another in desperation, almost as if they were one person.

Ani B finally broke free. "No, I must go; I have already made this decision." Everyone in the tent gathered around Yeshe to comfort the weeping girl. Ani B turned back to her sister. "Don't cry, sister; don't make everyone doubt us. I am going."

Stepping outside of the tent, Ani B stifled a sob. She had had to remove herself from her sister for fear she would lose her nerve. For the remainder of the night, she sat outside the tent in which her traveling companions were sleeping. Little by little, they began to wake and then invited Ani B inside. Seeing that she didn't have enough food, they filled her pack with butter, tsampa, and churi. As they walked past the tent where she had left her sister hours before, Ani B was overcome with tears. She thought about how her sister might be feeling, and hoped she was sleeping and not crying.

The walk down the mountain was difficult in the dark, with no moon to guide them across the uneven and rocky terrain. They came to a river as dawn began to break, and Ani B fondly remembered her sister's complaint so many weeks ago. *Ah, here is yet another river!* The group formed a chain, with Ani B and another nun in the center and the strongest people on the outside. "Now, hold on to each other and don't let go," Penpa warned them. "The river is cold and moving very fast." The women's long chubas quickly became heavy with water, making it difficult for them to move and maintain their grip on each other. In a moment, their hands slipped from each other's grasp. Ani B immediately thought, *Today I die; my life is finished.*

Calling out the names of the Dalai Lama and Karmapa, she heard a voice: "Don't be discouraged. Be strong; be strong; try to find each other's hands; hold on." Everyone shouted encouragement until the women's hands finally found each other again. Safely across the river, Ani B collapsed on the bank. Her sheepskin-and-wool chuba was soaking wet and so heavy that she could barely lift her body off the ground to walk.

From Mt. Kailash, the pilgrims walked to Lake Manasarovar, the next of the many sacred sites they would visit over the next several weeks on their way to India. Known to Tibetans as Mapam Yutso, the famed freshwater lake stands at an altitude of 15,100 feet and covers about 55 square miles, with a depth of 330 feet. The brilliant-blue water draws pilgrims from many religions—but it is not to be bathed in, though it can be collected for sacred rituals. Many religions in the region, including Hinduism, Jainism, Buddhism, and Tibet's pre-Buddhist religion, Bön, consider Manasarovar sacred, and it is visited yearly by many who are devout in their religious pursuits.

Arriving at the lake, Ani B and her group of friends were relieved to find themselves alone. They had time to take a break, make tea, and dry their clothes while napping in the warm sun. Unfortunately, Ani B had a bad case of diarrhea; her stomach was such a grumbling mess that while everyone else was relaxing and happy, she was in her own private hell. Feeling discouraged, her thoughts turned to her dearest sister, wondering if Yeshe had already left on her journey home. With a pang of regret, she wondered if maybe she had made a mistake and should have returned home with her sister. Pangs of regret and grief would appear unbidden throughout the next months as Ani B traveled further away from her sister, and home.

The small troupe visited holy places and monasteries in the area for the next two months. Often in exchange for chanting and prayers, they were given food and sometimes money. Both pairs of Ani B's shoes became threadbare; four months of continual walking had worn holes in the bottoms and her toes jutted through the front; repairs were fruitless. She was exhausted and weak, and yet spent thirteen days circumambulating a holy site near a monastery the group stayed in. Her commitment was relentless.

Rather than by a snakehead, her group was led by Penpa, the seventy-year-old monk who had made this same journey several times. His age was a concern for some in the group, who were not accustomed to such active seniors. Penpa assured everyone he was strong and healthy and quite capable of continuing; after all, only he knew the way into Nepal. Upon completing yet another circumambulation around a sacred site, he announced that they would leave for Nepal the next day, and that it was not far away. Two days later they arrived at the safe house, where Ani B and her friends were able to rest, eat, and regain some of their strength. Ani B's emotions and thoughts were a jumble during this time. She missed her sister as well as her father and grandmother. She missed the comfort of knowing the place she had been born and had grown up in. Seeing so many of the holiest sites and performing kora over the last months had been satisfying spiritually, but she longed for the comfort of her family. Though her thoughts frequently drifted to her family, she endeavored to find comfort in a restful place for a few days, with a steady supply of food and time to heal her aching body. One day, while resting in the sun and chatting with Penpa, an elderly Tibetan woman approached them. She questioned them about what was happening in Tibet. "Can we go back now? How is my house? When can we go back?" Tears coursed down her cheeks; clearly, all she wanted was to return to the life she once had in Tibet. Ani B and Penpa made futile attempts to reassure her, but in truth there was nothing that could be said. Tibet would never be as it once was.

Aside from the physical hardship of traveling by foot for many months—and well over 1,500 miles, without counting circumambulations—Ani B wasn't tested by negative human interaction. No one betrayed her or endangered her life. She arrived in Kathmandu dirty, feet blistered, exhausted, with her clothes full of fleas, but safe and satisfied that she had completed that part of the journey. Upon arrival at the refugee transit center, Ani B and her companions were advised sternly that they must wash their clothes and take showers. They were filthy and flea-bitten, and no one could stand the smell of them in such a state. Being concerned about the lives of those tiny but pesky fleas, Ani B refused to wash her chuba and instead placed it outside, hoping the critters would leave of their own accord. On that first night, she and another nun went to the shower room together. Neither had a clue how to use the shower. Instead, they laughed from embarrassment at being naked in front of each other and feeling foolish in this new technology, which they had never in their lives experienced. The next night, Ani B advised the woman that they should go separately to the shower to avoid their crippling embarrassment. After so many months without bathing, Ani B luxuriated in the water and soap, collapsing into bed renewed and relaxed. With new clothing given to her by the center, she burned the tattered shoes and other garments she had worn under her chuba. Eventually, Ani B got the hang of the shower and became fastidious, showering every day. Without her blood to feast on, the fleas departed from her chuba, and after cleaning it she somehow managed to send it back to Yeshe in Tibet.

Ani B and her companions quickly became bastions of cleanliness. The squat toilets were a horror when they arrived—so bad in fact that Ani B vomited from the stench and filthy condition. "Better to go outside in a bush than be in the awful smell of the toilet!" The only solution was to clean the toilet herself. Enlisting the help of her traveling companions, they did just that. Every day they cleaned, and they began encouraging others to be careful and clean after themselves. Soon, the toilets were as clean as could be. Ani B and her friends also began helping in the kitchen, cooking thukpa and momos and helping to keep everything clean and orderly. After a month, the center administration honored the band of companions during one of the meals as exemplary models of cleanliness. Ani B was embarrassed but proud.

After a couple of months at the refugee center in Kathmandu, Ani B and her companions were bussed to the Tibetan Reception Center in Delhi. Like so many before her, she was sick from the bus ride, and then later sick from the food, smells, and water in India. Seeing she was miserable, Penpa arranged for her to travel to Bir with him, the Tibetan settlement where he had many friends and family. At Bir, just three hours south of Dharamsala, Ani B was able to rest, gain strength and begin to assess what life in India held for her. As her body responded to regular sleep, and proper food, and surrounded by Tibetans who had settled into life in India, her outlook on her situation brightened. Maybe she had made the correct choice after all.

Penpa suggested to Ani B that they travel further south to the holy city of Bodhgaya, the place of the Buddha's enlightenment under the Bodhi tree. There, they would participate in both the Kagyu and Gelug Mönlam prayer festival. Visiting Bodhgaya was a turning point for Ani B. The hardships of illness and physical exertion, missing her sister and family—any doubts that had nagged at her during the long pilgrimage dissolved. Deeply moved by the spiritual experiences there, she thought, *Now my life has meaning*.

Like all pilgrims who leave Tibet, there was one more thing she had to do: visit the Dalai Lama. On the appointed day, she rose in the early morning, recited prayers for an hour, ate balep—Tibetan bread—and drank tea. After doing a kora around the Dalai Lama's temple, she lined up to meet him. Waiting patiently in the small room as so many had before her, Ani B imagined asking him so many questions, basking in his presence, being near him, having a good chat. After he had spoken to the group, the time came to offer khatas. As each Tibetan filed past, offering the ceremonial scarf, Ani B stood trembling, slightly bowed, eyes cast down, but occasionally sneaking a glance at him. When it was her turn, she offered her khata, with tears streaming down her face. The Dalai Lama took the white scarf, placed it over the back of her neck, and held her hand for a moment. He said a blessing, and then someone was pulling at her to move on. She resisted, thinking, *What is happening? I am not done; why is this person pulling me?* Wanting to stay longer in the presence of His Holiness the Fourteenth Dalai Lama, she continued to resist the pull. Then someone whispered in her ear: "Ani, you must move on so others can meet him too." His Holiness nodded to her and then she realized what was happening. There would be no chat, no questions for him to answer; reluctant yet satisfied, she shuffled out of the room.

Eventually, Ani B arrived at a nunnery in Nepal, where she stayed for a brief time. There, she shaved off her hair for the first time and learned what it was to be in a cloistered situation. She found it stifling. Instead, she decided she would take a retreat. Leaving the nunnery, she found a place of seclusion, and for three years prayed and meditated. Emerging from the retreat, Ani B's hair had grown to her waist, and she saw no reason to shave it. Hair or no hair, she was a devotee of the Buddhist faith. During her chosen solitude, she decided to take up residence in McLeodganj. Being near the Dalai Lama, the Karmapa, and the mountains felt right to her.

By this time, cell phone use was the norm, and she was able to communicate with her family. One day, she learned that her sister was trying to get a passport and visa to visit India. Ani B was thrilled at the news, and immediately began making plans for all the sacred sites she would show Yeshe. Her little sister would become a nun like her, and they would live happily in McLeodganj. She imagined all the trips they would take to holy Buddhist sites, praying, and once again living together. It was nearly all she could think about every day.

A few months later, the bad news arrived. Yeshe, unable to get a visa, was to marry instead. Her father delivered the edict and thus Yeshe had no say in the matter. Ani B was devastated. So eager to reunite with Yeshe, she had gotten her hopes up. The news unseated her, and she wept for days on end. In Ani B's thinking, Yeshe would never again be free. Her sister would become a servant to her husband, and eventually children, and have no freedom. In her grief and despair, she was unable to eat or sleep. After weeks of this, a nun friend came to visit her. Sternly, she admonished Ani B for such behavior. "Why are you crying? Nothing happened to your sister. Nothing is wrong; she is only getting married." Grief was really the culprit in Ani B's despair. She had given up so much to realize her dreams and had clung to the notion that Yeshe would one day join her in India. She had allowed herself to believe that the pain of her sister's absence would be healed at their reunion. The news of Yeshe's impending marriage had put an end to that possibility.

Several years later, Ani B was able to get permission to return to Tibet to visit her family. Reunion with Yeshe was joyous. Meeting her sister's children and husband reassured Ani B that Yeshe's life had turned out exactly as it should have. Ani B was an aunt, and she indulged the children and her sister with affection. She relished the time she spent with her sister in Tibet, but she realized she could not stay. India and the monastic community were now her home. Satisfied that her sister was happy with her life in Tibet, Ani B couldn't ask for more.

After living in India for nearly twenty years, Ani B embarked on a new adventure. Contrary to the advice she had once given her sister, Ani B married a Tibetan man living in Canada and emigrated there to be with him. She is no longer Ani B; now, she is Bhuti. Her hair is still long, but she no longer wears the maroon garb of a nun. She does, however, read scripture every morning, continuing her devotion to the Buddhist faith. Yeshe is still in Tibet, where she has five children. Bhuti is as bright a spirit as she always was. She appreciates her life in the modernity of Canada, is working full-time in a luxury hotel making sure rooms are spotless and ready for each guest, and has adjusted well to a very different world than the one from which she came.

NUNS, MONKS, AND VOWS

In Tibetan Buddhism, it is customary for both monks and nuns to shave their heads as a symbol of renunciation. However, there are some exceptions, notably the Jomo (Jetsunma) tradition most notable in parts of eastern Tibet, where some nuns—especially highly realized practitioners or hermits—may choose to keep their hair long or partially shaved. Like Ani B during her three-year retreat, nuns and monks allow their hair to grow, rather than being distracted by the effort of physical attention. In some regions, yoginis or female practitioners following esoteric or non-monastic tantric paths may keep their hair as a sign of their specific vows or practices. However, these cases are relatively rare, and not the norm within the larger Tibetan Buddhist monastic tradition.

Though nuns have been involved in Tibetan Buddhism since its seventh-century origins, due to the patriarchal nature of monastic life, the devotion of nuns to Buddhism was largely obscured until the late twentieth century. A push for equity among male and female monastics has seen more nuns gain prominence in Tibetan Buddhism. The Dalai Lama has been an advocate of women gaining higher levels of education, and thus recognition. In his estimation, the more people that practice the Buddha Dharma (teaching), the greater the benefit to all. He believes women are equal to men—if not more capable—in this endeavor. Traditionally, only monks were eligible to train for the geshe degree, the highest achievable study in the Gelugpa sect of Tibetan Buddhism. Nuns were not allowed to undertake this level of PhD-equivalent study until 2012. Since then, and with the Dalai Lama's encouragement and their own hard work, seventy-three nuns have earned the female geshema degree as of 2023. Seventeen years of study are required, and at least a 75-percent score in those studies, to qualify to sit for the geshema exam. The study is rigorous, including four years of written work, debates, defending their chosen thesis, and a final twelve-day exam. Receiving this degree allows the nuns to teach and hold various leadership positions in their communities, and is a sign of women's increasing value in what has traditionally been a patriarchal culture.

The Tibetan Nuns Project (TNP), a non-profit founded in 1987, supports seven nunneries in the Himalayan region—Dolma Ling Nunnery and Institute, Shugsep Nunnery and Institute, Geden Choeling Nunnery, Tilokpur Nunnery, Sakya College for Nuns, Sherab Choeling Nunnery, and Dorjee Zong Nunnery. The organization receives financial support from Buddhist donors the world over and has supported hundreds of nuns in their quest for Buddhist education. Many of the nuns emerging from these and other nunneries go on to become leaders and teachers in the Buddhist tradition. Thirty years of sustained support via the TNP has done much to ensure that the Tibetan religion and culture remain robust.

One Tibetan nunnery not supported by TNP is Dongyu Gatsal Ling Nunnery, founded by Jetsunma (Venerable Master) Tenzin Palmo. Born in England in 1943, Tenzin Palmo discovered Buddhism as a young woman, and at the age of twenty-one sailed to India to begin her serious pursuit of Buddhist study. Diane Perry, as she was named at birth, became one of the first Westerners to be ordained as a Buddhist monastic. After twelve years of intensive study in northern India, she sought to live in seclusion to practice with few interruptions. Her devotion to the spiritual practice was so intense that she sought out a cave not far from Tayul Monastery in northern India, adapted it to her needs, and spent the next twelve years living mostly secluded. In 1999, she began the foundations for Dongyu Gatsal Ling Nunnery in Kangra District, Himachal Pradesh, which now provides Buddhist education to 100 nuns.

Rebuilding the Tibetan monastic tradition in India after the Dalai Lama's escape in 1959 was a long and arduous process. Among the original 80,000 Tibetans that streamed across the Himalayas following the Dalai Lama's exile in India were many of Tibet's most renowned scholars, spiritual masters, reincarnated Lamas, and young monk students from all four Tibetan sects of Buddhism—Gelugpa, Nyingma, Sakya, and Kagyu—as well as the Bön tradition. Like many Tibetan refugees at that time, their condition was thought to be temporary. It was believed that they would be able to return to their homes and monasteries in Tibet in a short time. As we now know, that was not to be.

As the political reality of Tibet's situation began to sink in, the Dalai Lama feared the great tradition of Tibetan Buddhism would die out without centralizing the study and teaching of these important traditions. Tibetan refugees, including monks and nuns, had been put to work building roads in a variety of areas in India to provide employment to these mostly unskilled agrarians and monastics. This meant that the time and devotion required to study Buddhism were under threat. At the Dalai Lama's urging, then-Prime Minister of India Jawaharlal Nehru agreed to provide access to locations where monks and nuns could continue their studies. One such area was a former British prison camp in West Bengal called Buxa Duar, which the Tibetans renamed Buxa Chogar—the Dharma camp at Buxa. It was here that 1,500 Tibetan monks and nuns from three of the four sects of Tibetan Buddhism lived and studied together for the next decade, a first in Tibetan history. The conditions were unsanitary, and the Tibetans were not accustomed to the humidity and heat. Many died from tuberculosis, dysentery, and malaria; those who survived continued to study after Buxar closed in 1969. Eventually, many who had studied at Buxar went on to teach at other monasteries and nunneries that were being re-established throughout India.

Between 1959 and 1970, over 6,000 monasteries were destroyed in Tibet as part of the Cultural Revolution carried out by China's Red Guards. Some of those monasteries have since been rebuilt, but many remain in ruins. As of late 2020, there were 281 Tibetan Buddhist monasteries and nunneries in India. Most of these are situated along the Indo-Himalayan border and play a significant role in the cultural and spiritual life of local communities. These institutions continue to preserve and promote Tibetan Buddhist traditions and education in India.

To accommodate the large influx of Tibetan exiles to India in the decades following 1959, the monk refugees inhabited existing monasteries in India and over time new ones were built. The Namdrolling Monastery, also known as the Golden Temple, was established in 1963 and is one of the largest teaching centers of the Nyingma tradition. Drepung Loseling Monastery was re-established in 1963, after the original was destroyed in Tibet. In 1970, Sera Monastery was also re-established after its destruction in Tibet. Both Drepung and Sera follow the Gelug tradition, and serve as major centers for Buddhist learning. Ganden Monastery of the Gulgpa sect of Tibetan Buddhism was also destroyed in Tibet, and was rebuilt in India during the 1960s. The Dalai Lama's personal monastery, Namgyal, was re-established beginning in 1959, after his arrival in India. The Tsuglagkhang Complex, which encompasses the Namgyal Monastery, temples, a large courtyard, a museum, and living quarters, is a major Tibetan Buddhist institution that was slowly built through the 1960s and 1970s as time and funds became available. The Namgyal Monastery hosts over 200 monks and the complex is a gathering place for Tibetans, Indians, and Buddhist practitioners from around the world who come to hear the Dalai Lama's teachings or celebrate specific occasions, like the Dalai Lama's birthday or the yearly March 10 Uprising Commemoration. Visitors spin prayer wheels inside and outside of the complex, perform prostrations, and visit the two temples.

Today, there are roughly 30,000 Tibetan monks and nuns living in thriving monastic communities across India. Like Ani B, some do choose to leave the monastic life for a variety of reasons. While a deeply personal decision, it is generally accepted within Tibetan Buddhist culture. The lure of a romantic partnership and parenthood can be a powerful force that often compels monks or nuns to integrate into secular society. Modern influences likely play a role in shifting perspectives on monastic commitment, leading to the choice to disrobe and adopt a more mainstream lifestyle. Living an austere life, especially in India, can be challenging. Not all monasteries and nunneries provide lifelong financial security, which increases hardship when facing healthcare issues, aging, or the needs of the extended family. Sometimes individuals may find that the monastic life no longer aligns with their personal spiritual journey for a variety of reasons. Those who enter the monastic life as very young children are exposed to the modern influences of internet access, social media, and the wider world in general, propelling some to choose a less ascetic life. For some, health, extended family, and the need for financial security create pressure to leave the rigor of the monastic life and pursue other avenues. Even as lay people, most remain true to the practice of Buddhism in their daily lives. Monastic life has its challenges even in India, and the lure of consumerism, romance, and influences of the modern-day world can be difficult to resist, especially in McLeodganj, where visitors from around the world mingle with the monastic population daily. Gone are the days of seclusion in the remote reaches of Tibet or India that once protected the monastic life from outside influences.

CHAPTER 4

THE LONG PILGRIMAGE

Dechen fondly recalls the idyllic early years of her childhood. Her mother, a nomad woman named Tsering, gave birth to Dechen at the age of thirty, sometime in the early 1980s. They lived with Tsering's mother in a black tent made of yak wool, moving with the seasons and grazing their animals across the vast Tibetan Plateau. Dechen's grandmother was in such poor health that she was unable to assist with the chores, so Tsering cared for over 150 animals by herself. Dechen helped as much as possible, though she was quite young. However, having endured a horrific childhood herself, Tsering demanded very little of her young daughter. Instead, she dreamed of a better life for Dechen, and was determined to ensure her one and only daughter was protected and loved.

Life as a nomad in the valleys and the hillsides beneath the great mountains was full of adventure, and in Dechen's memory remains colored by the perceptions of a young girl who believed in ghosts and monsters. Because Dechen hasn't seen Tibet in many years, her memories are cemented, rooted in the fancies of a child's miraculous wonder. During the three seasons of nomadic movement, she vividly recalls wildly racing horses with the other nomad children across the endless expanse of the plateau, or foraging for mushrooms, and following the animals. Winters were spent in a small earthen home watching her mother spin wool and make clothing. Dechen was too young to perceive or remember hardship; instead, she remembers only freedom and joy, and longs to return to the land of her birth.

A scattering of black tents, including that of Tsering's older brother, dotted the valley where they lived for most of the grazing season. Knowing his sister was alone with many animals to care for, in addition to an aging parent and a young daughter, he would often send one of his elder children to help Tsering. Each family was responsible for its own animals and members, yet a communal attitude ensured that no one suffered hardship without the help and camaraderie of other nomads. Throughout the summer months, nomad families would often gather for picnics and bonfires, and Dechen often had playmates to run wild with. Her face lights up as she recalls those memories—especially of riding horses. Laughing, she recounts renting a horse in India and immediately spurring the animal into a full run, with her whooping what sounded like a war cry, much to the shock and dismay of the owners, who attempted to give chase. Such is the spirit of Dechen.

Dechen is quick with a smile, a laugh, and the willingness to press on, regardless of her situation. Even as an adult, she is not above climbing trees or jumping from them, to the astonishment of those around her. Dechen is playful but hard-working. Teaching the Tibetan language at an immersion school in McLeodganj, she is dedicated to her Western students. Unlike their teacher, Dechen's students are privileged by the fortune of birth and belonging. Citizenship and passports allow her students the freedom of movement across the world, while Dechen is confined to India and Nepal. A Chinese visa has repeatedly eluded her, making her homeland seem an impossible destination. Yet she firmly believes her salvation will come from positive thinking and prayer, and so she lives between three worlds: the past of her idyllic childhood, a life in limbo in India, and a hopeful future.

Staying busy keeps her mind occupied and prevents the nagging worries and doubts about her future and her mother's health that creep in during the silence of night. Dechen is enterprising as well. While teaching the Tibetan language, she also learned to drive a car, became licensed, and began a side hustle teaching others to drive. From that money, she started a tsampa-making endeavor, roasting the barley grains, grinding them into flour, and selling the end product by the pound to local Tibetans.

Dechen's mother and grandmother suffered through the early years of China's occupation of Tibet. Their experiences are formative of Dechen's identity, even though she was born after the worst of the suffering. For nearly three decades after the Communist Party (CCP) took control of China, it kept its borders—including occupied Tibet—closed off from the wider world. During the 1980s, China began to open up, and some of the strict controls in Tibet were loosened. Tibet emerged from isolation as much a mysterious land to Westerners as it had been decades earlier, but with the tremendous destruction brought on by Mao's disastrous Great Leap Forward, which resulted in the deaths of thousands of people from starvation. Instead of feeding a nation, Mao's policies brought hardship and famine. The Cultural Revolution that followed and the destroying of the *"four olds"*—ideas, culture, habits, and customs—turned 6,000 of Tibet's monasteries into rubble in an attempt to obliterate Tibet's adherence to Buddhism and the monastic tradition. Replacing the Tibetan theocracy, Communists became the governors of Tibetan lives and their futures. But although the Tibetan way of life had been disrupted by years of brutal and unnecessary hardship, the Tibetan culture was not yet destroyed. Tibet's reopening in the mid-1980s revealed that Tibetans were worse off than they had been prior to the Communist takeover. Yet many continued to live as they always had, though instead of being relatively carefree to live their lives as they chose, the Communists had left them with the grief of unspeakable loss and destruction, under the ever-watchful eye of the CCP.

From her perspective as a young girl, the years of tumult had no discernable effect on Dechen's remote nomadic life on the Tibetan Plateau. Not until much later did she become aware of China and the surrounding geopolitical influences. Her mother had seen no need to burden her young daughter with tails of her own traumatic experiences of the occupation. Tsering and her mother had endured the turbulent early years of the Chinese invasion and the ensuing famine and cultural destruction. Tibetan life had been turned upside down by military violence, rebellion, arrests, torture, starvation, death, imprisonment, labor camps, and long separation from family members, or the loss of family completely. Years later, when Dechen was old enough, Tsering began to share stories with her daughter, and this awareness of her mother's early life and the abuse her family had experienced is an important part of Dechen's identity, influencing the dedicated care and unending patience she exhibits in caring for her now-aging mother.

While not widely known, the story of Tibetan resistance played a key role early in Dechen's mother's life, in the early 1960s. Due to their proximity to China's border, for years the Khampas of eastern Tibet, where Dechen's family is from, fought a guerilla war against the People's Liberation Army (PLA). The defiant Khampa rebellion brought much attention to the villages and nomads of the eastern provinces. Many of Dechen's relatives were involved in the early resistance; many were killed or arrested and sent to labor camps, like Tsering and her mother. Born in 1951, Tsering had lived through the worst years in Tibet, when the Chinese forced Communist ideologies and reforms on citizens. Forcibly separated from her family as an eight-year-old, Tsering had been forced into labor with other children, gathering wood, yak dung, and rocks in a labor camp. When she was thirteen, she was sent to live and work at an agricultural collective raising animals,[1] again by force. After seventeen years of separation, not knowing if her family were still alive, Tsering was reunited with her mother and brother. Her mother had been tortured, beaten, forced into hard labor, and starved, like so many others during the early years of Mao's regime. She and Tsering both carried the many scars of cruelty and depravation they had endured, some visible and some, such as Tsering's mother, that crippled them physically and mentally. She would never be the same mother Tsering had known in the first eight years of her life.

After so many years forced to work against her will, Tsering was finally free to own and raise her own animals. Despite having to care for her crippled mother, young Dechen, and many animals, she persisted with fierce resolve. Having received some education during her time in the labor camps, Tsering understood the importance of education for her daughter. Like many parents, she tried to provide a better life for Dechen, and knew that the plateau was not the place to find an education for her daughter. But India was. As Dechen grew, Tsering became increasingly determined to better her daughter's life. Tsering had become a deeply religious woman, and she wanted to go on a pilgrimage—an important undertaking that she believed would bring merit and virtue. But the responsibility of caring for her aging and crippled mother, her young daughter, and so many animals kept her tied to the nomadic life.

Dechen was nine when her grandmother died. Heartbreaking though it was to lose her mother for good, Tsering was relieved her mother no longer suffered in horrible and debilitating pain. She also knew this was her chance to make the changes to her life that she had envisioned. Tsering and her brother arranged for their mother's body to undergo the traditional sky burial, and then she began making her plans to embark on a pilgrimage with her daughter. A year later, she decisively took all the animals to her brother's encampment and, though he protested mightily, Tsering walked away from nomadic life and onto the path of a spiritual pilgrim.

Over the course of the next two years, Dechen and her mother traversed Tibet, from Kham to Lhasa, and visited Mt. Kailash three times. They visited a host of sacred sites and monasteries in between, camped in wide-open spaces, and stayed with friends and relatives, in monasteries, and in strangers' homes. Never having ventured far from her mother's side and the safety of the familiar nomad lands, Dechen was afraid of a great many things as she walked away from the remote and wild area she was accustomed to. Tsering, however, was nearly fearless. All that she had experienced growing up had toughened her; there was very little that she hadn't seen or experienced that could unseat her. Her mother's confidence helped Dechen feel safe for the most part.

From the distance of age and maturity, Dechen laughs at her childish fears and brims with anecdotes of her foolishness and the two-year adventure she and her mother boldly undertook. A favorite story is the first time she saw a truck. A week or so after leaving their nomad home, she and her mother were walking near a road. From a distance, Dechen heard a rumbling sound. As it grew louder, the earth beneath her feet vibrated lightly, and in the distance a dust cloud moved toward them. Alarmed and fearful, Dechen looked to her mother for guidance, who only chuckled at her daughter's ignorance.

"What is it?" Dechen asked her mother.

"Motor," she replied.

"Motor?"

When Dechen saw the large, growling truck approaching, streaming dust in its wake, she bolted in the opposite direction, terrified of the strange beast bearing down on them. As Dechen ran, she turned to make sure her mother was following; instead, Tsering was nearly busting at the seams with laughter.

"Dechen!" she shouted, 'Come here; there is nothing to be afraid of, it is only iron, not a monster." Thinking her mother must have gone mad, Dechen remained firmly planted far from the approaching truck, watching in horror as the roaring dust cloud approached her mother. When the truck passed by harmlessly, Dechen slowly walked back to where her mother stood, bent over with laughter.

Later, Dechen got a close-up inspection of an iron monster. Her mother encouraged her to climb on the truck's tires and into the back to feel its cold, hard sides. "See, it's just iron, nothing to be afraid of. It's not alive, but the tires move, so be careful." Previously viewed as a monster, the motor became a wondrous form of transportation. With wind blowing through her hair, Dechen stood tall in the back of each truck they had an opportunity to ride in, surveying the passing landscape with delight.

The remote life of a nomad had sheltered her from so much of the wider world. At nearly every turn Dechen was exposed to and challenged by new sights, people, things, and tastes. Arriving in Lhasa, she was overwhelmed by the size and number of buildings, the activity of vehicles, and the people everywhere. When the sun went down and the lights of the city appeared, Dechen mistook them for stars, and had difficulty understanding the concept of electricity, which she had never seen. On this first visit to the holy city, a large celebration filled the streets with brightly dressed people, balloons, and music. Transfixed by the gaiety and color, Dechen could only stare, mouth agape. When children ran up to her and handed her candy, she wondered why they were giving her things. For the first time in her life, she began to make comparisons between herself and others. Her ragged, dirty clothes against the beautiful colored silks the children wore brought feelings of discomfort she had not known before. The poor and crippled people in Lhasa begging for money affected her most of all. Never had she seen anyone missing a leg or hand and she was so deeply affected she couldn't stop crying. Unaware of her own poverty, she asked her mother for money for these unfortunate souls, and patiently waited for her to dig a coin out from the depths of her chuba.

Another oddity in Dechen's arsenal of new sights, sounds, and experiences were the many foreigners. Some had skin and hair colors unlike any she had seen before, and she found it hard not to stare. Taking pity on the scruffy child one man saw before him, he handed Dechen a box of cooked chicken. She didn't know what a chicken was, had never seen or eaten one. After looking inside the box, she whispered in horror, "Mother, are these children's legs?"

Again, Tsering chuckled at her daughter. "No, it is a bird called chicken. Many people eat this."

"Will you eat, mother?"

"No, I am too old to try new things, but you can try this. Someday, you will live where people eat like this, and you must know how."

For Dechen, nothing could have been less appetizing than food that reminded her of human baby legs. She had only known the horses, yaks, and sheep her mother had kept, and wild animals such as antelope, cranes, bears, and small rodents roaming freely on the plateau.

"I can't eat it, mother."

"That's okay, but don't throw it out."

Spying a young boy nearby who appeared equally impoverished, Dechen gave him the strange food. Clearly more amenable to cooked legs, he did not hesitate to begin ravenously eating the proffered food.

After a year of crisscrossing from one holy site to another, Dechen and her mother returned to their former nomad home in eastern Tibet. Tsering sold all the animals to the other nomad families and her brother. She donated most of the proceeds to the nearby monastery, keeping only a small amount for herself. Tsering was ready to walk away from her nomadic life and to send Dechen to India to receive an education from one of the Tibetan boarding schools. She did not at that point inform Dechen of her plan. Instead, mother and daughter embarked on another yearlong pilgrimage.

Toward the end of that year, while circumambulating Mt. Kailash, Tsering met a man named Nygma, who had arranged for a small group of people to cross the mountains into India. He was sure the guide he had hired would welcome Dechen to travel with them. By this time, Dechen was nearly thirteen years old, and in her mother's thinking old enough to handle such a journey—and well past time to begin an education. While Tsering spoke of the many holy Rinpoches in India, such as the Dalai Lama, and the many monasteries there, Nygma showed Dechen pictures of beautiful flowers, sacred temples, mountains, and other things she couldn't understand but thought she would like to see. Tsering began to explain to Dechen her plan to send her to India to live at a special school for Tibetan children.

"By myself, mother, without you?"

"Yes, dear, it will be very good for your future."

Dechen made it very clear that this idea was out of the question. "I will not go by myself. What if I don't like it—what will happen to me? I will have no one."

Clearly, Dechen had absorbed some of her mother's determination. Tsering looked long and hard at her spirited yet frightened and tearful daughter, thinking of her own childhood, filled with unhappiness and loss. She remembered how painful it had been when she was separated from her own mother and realized she could not do the same to Dechen. Knowing it was the right thing to do, Tsering relented to Dechen's pleas. Mother and daughter would cross the mountains together.

Nygma introduced Tsering and Dechen to the small group of Tibetans they would travel with. The adults spoke in hushed tones over a campfire and food, telling stories of arrests and torture, thieves stealing money and clothes, and worse. These stories made Dechen concerned about many things, but also about where to hide their money. Later in the night, Dechen showed her mother how they could open the large end of the toothpaste tube, put money in, and roll it back up. Tsering humored her inventive daughter and also hid money in the patches of their chubas.

A few nights later, Dechen awoke to Nygma and another man standing in the tent, wearing backpacks. Tsering had shaken her lightly to wake up. It was time to go. Leaving the tent behind as a decoy, mother and daughter followed the men out into the night and began a long jog to a river. There, the rest of the group waited for them. As usual, the group would move only at night, and this first night they needed to move quickly to put distance between themselves and Mt. Kailash. Stumbling in the dark, Dechen had difficulty keeping up with the adults, and Tsering held her hand, keeping her steady as they jogged along. Sometime later, Dechen, her mother, and two others realized they had lost the rest of the group. It was so dark that they couldn't see.

"Where is everyone?"

No one could answer definitively where the others had gone, or in which direction. The two men, Tenzin and Palden, wanted to go and find the remaining group. Tsering cautioned, "No, it's too dark; we can't see anything. Better to stay here tonight and look in the morning." Reluctantly the men agreed, and the four settled down on the cold, hard ground for the night.

In the morning, from the top of a foothill, they had a perfect view of the expanse of land between them and the brilliant blue of Lake Manasarovar, cutting a visible swath through the barren distance. Dechen's mother claimed there was a path far, far off ahead of them. "Maybe that is where the others are," she explained. Tenzin and Palden strained to see but could not make out a path.

"There is nothing there; you are seeing things, sister."

"It is there; I know because I have lots of experience and know how to look." The men were skeptical but decided to follow her anyway.

The four travelers headed for the sacred lake. In Tibetan belief, all sacred sites must be circumambulated in a clockwise direction; to do otherwise is considered disrespectful and could bring negative circumstances to one's life. However, to properly circumambulate the lake to end up where Tsering believed they should be would require two full days of walking. Walking counterclockwise would put them where they wanted to be in half a day. Tsering consulted with Tenzin and Palden, who agreed to take the chance of circumambulating in the wrong direction in the hope that no one would discover them. But after a couple of hours, they came upon a Tibetan man, who suspiciously questioned what they were doing.

"We are pilgrims taking kora around the holy lake," said Palden.

The man immediately responded, "Why are you lying? I am Tibetan, you are Tibetan; do not tell lies."

Tsering jumped in quickly to explain. "We are going to Nepal and have lost the rest of our group. Please don't tell anyone about us."

He examined the four companions carefully, as if measuring their worth, and then assured Tsering that he would keep their secret. "There is a small monastery not far from here. You can get food and rest, but be careful—there are often Chinese police there."

Because a mother and daughter would cause less suspicion if there were police at the monastery, Tsering informed Tenzin and Palden that she and Dechen would go and beg for food. The men were not happy with this outspoken woman giving direction, but with Tsering's firm stance on the matter, they finally relented. Being so near to Lake Manasarovar and Mt. Kailash, it was not unusual for pilgrims to stop at the monastery to ask for food or help. The monk whom Tsering and Dechen met when they arrived was not surprised to see a woman and a child in the courtyard.

"Where are you going?" he asked.

Tsering confided that they were going to India. "Will you do a divination for us? Will we be successful?"

Shaking his head, he replied, "Oh, I am not good at this. I will pray for you instead."

She insisted he must do a divination anyway. "Good or not, you must do this for us."

Somewhat exasperated, he agreed, saying, "If I am right and the divination is good, you must go the way I tell you. There will be fewer problems for you. But don't tell anyone; police are always coming here asking us questions."

The monk produced a set of mo dice from a small pouch in the depths of his chuba, then carefully threw them across a long table. He confidently announced, "Your journey will be successful, though you may have some problems too."

Returning to Tenzin and Palden, Tsering and Dechen shared the food and tea and Tsering gave them the directions from the monk. But the two men had formulated their own plan and refused to listen to her, despite the information having come from a monk at the monastery. They'd had enough of this bossy woman, and headed off in the opposite direction. Thinking them foolish, Tsering and Dechen followed the monk's advice and walked in the direction he advised. Once again, it was dark and difficult to see. Dechen stumbled repeatedly, but her mother held tight to her hand, preventing her from falling or straying off the path. At some point, Dechen saw what appeared to be the shape of a human coming toward them. Her skin prickled and she lost all sense of her feet touching the ground.

"Mother, is it a ghost?"

"No, no there are no ghosts here, Dechen-la."

A voice called to them, "Where are the others?"

Tsering explained the situation to the man, who had been sent to find them.

"Ah leh, ah leh," he said wearily, "we must go and find them." Norbu, the tall Tibetan Dechen thought had been a ghost, moved off in the direction of the two errant men, quickly found them, and then led the group for two more hours before making camp for the night.

The next morning, Nygma appeared, seemingly out of nowhere. "I have been so worried about you," he said, taking Tsering's backpack; "I have been looking for you for two days now."

Dechen felt a sense of relief now that Nygma was in their midst again. She was tired from the long night of walking, and while the adults prepared food and tea, she laid down on the ground to sleep. By mid-morning, Tsering was gently shaking Dechen once again. It was time to go. They were to meet with the guide Nygma had hired. To keep pace with the fast-moving men, Tsering took Dechen's backpack and stayed close to her, with encouragement to keep her eyes ahead of her; it would only be a little bit farther. From her chuba she handed Dechen some tea leaves, explaining that if she chewed on them, it would give her energy—"But don't swallow them; spit them out when you are done chewing." Dechen was thirsty and found it difficult to chew the dry leaves, and the bitter taste left her feeling thirstier than energized. After walking for several hours in the morning sun, Dechen longed to rest and sleep the weariness from her limbs. Yet, her mother encouraged her to keep moving. Eventually, Dechen spied a narrow column of smoke rising from the hill ahead of them. Suddenly, she found her hand being grasped firmly by a monk who in her sleep-deprived daze seemed to have appeared out of nowhere. He carefully helped her walk up the hill to where the guide and remaining group were sitting around a small fire, drinking tea and eating.

Finally able to rest and satisfy her thirst and growling stomach, Dechen was happy to rejoin the group. As she quietly observed the adults, she began to feel uneasy about the two newest people gathered around the small fire. One was to be their guide across the mountains into Nepal. He was loud and his language course, and Dechen decided she did not trust him. She wasn't sure whether or not he was Tibetan because he didn't dress or behave like anyone she knew, and though he spoke Tibetan, it sounded strange to her. She stayed as far away from him as possible. His wife was a different story. From Dechen's assessment, though very quiet and timid, she too was not to be trusted. As dusk descended, the group broke camp and began walking into the evening. There were fifteen people and this time they made every effort to stay together so no one would get lost in the dark.

Many days after leaving Mt. Kailash, the food supply had run low, and before entering a forested area they made a thin soup of tsampa to share. As they ate, the guide warned them that they must be very careful from now on; they had reached a dangerous area. During a brief sleep, Tsering had a terrible dream, and later told Dechen to stay very close to her: "Don't walk with anyone else." She wouldn't tell Dechen the details of her dream. Having lived a remote life, Dechen was wary of new people, or maybe it was intuition—either way, she continued to regard the guide and his wife with suspicion. When the guide's wife walked alongside her and gave her bits of candy, Dechen questioned her motivations. Like the children who had given her candy in Lhasa, she wondered, *What does she want?*

When the troupe came upon an old, abandoned house very near the Nepal border, they took advantage of the cover and slept inside for the day. The guide instructed his wife to go to the nearby village to buy beer for him. Tsering gave Dechen some coins to buy noodles if she could find any. Dechen continued to feel uncomfortable with the woman but obeyed her mother and set off with the guide's wife. The woman told Dechen she was afraid of her husband when he drank beer, so she would only buy a small amount. When Dechen and the guide's wife returned to the house with only half the amount of beer, her husband began to complain loudly.

"Why, why," he yelled, "why always only half the beer?!"

He was very angry, grumbled all through dinner, and was drunk by the time the rest of the group had settled in to sleep. Out of a deep sleep, Dechen woke suddenly to hear the husband and wife arguing. Sneaking a peek in their direction, she saw the guide hit his wife in the head. Someone turned on a flashlight and everyone started to intervene.

"Stop, stop! You mustn't hit her!" Tsering stepped in front of the guide, putting herself between him and his bleeding wife. She sternly advised him, "Do not do this to your wife. It is very bad karma for you."

"Why are you telling me what to do? Do you want this too?" he snarled back at her. With his fist raised, Tsering only looked at him dispassionately. Defiant as always, she didn't back down.

"If you want to hit me too, then do it."

Dechen started crying at this possibility and the guide turned his anger on her. "Why are you crying? Shut up!"

Dechen cowered under his angry gaze; she'd never seen anyone behave like this before. Two monks in the party attempted to diffuse the situation and calm the man down, who then began threatening everyone.

"If anyone tries to stop me, I will kill you."

He towered over most of the Tibetans in the group and, even while swaying drunkenly, was intimidating. Tsering ignored the man and instead turned her attention to caring for his wife's bleeding head wound. Eventually, the man wandered off and everyone was able to calm down and settle back to sleep. Dechen's dreams that night were filled with the altercation.

In the morning, the group was awakened by the guide's yelling: "Get up, get up! It's time to go! Hurry, the police will arrest us!"

No one was sure he was telling the truth, but they scrambled to gather belongings anyway. Tsering pulled Dechen aside. "Stay with the wife. He won't hurt her if you are with her."

"But why, mother? I don't want to walk with her."

"Just go now; it will be okay. I will watch you."

Reluctantly, Dechen fell in step with the guide's wife. Afraid the woman's face would be damaged from the blow she had received the night before, Dechen avoided looking directly at her and walked with her eyes cast down. During the rest break, Tsering helped the guide's wife wash the blood from her hair and then applied a special Tibetan medicine to the gash in her scalp. Having never seen a wound like this before, Dechen was deeply worried.

"Is she going to die, mother?"

"No dear, she will not."

After a day's hike, the group reached a snow-covered mountain. The guide knew of a path that would take them closer to Nepal and skirt the army camp at its base. Concerned about the danger of snow-blindness, the women cut some of their hair and made eyeshades to protect their eyes. The hair was matted and pliable, easily stretching across the eyes and hooking around the ears like a pair of sunglasses. During the process of making eyeshades, one of the monks accidently cut his arm badly. Dechen remembers her mother taking some lamb's wool from the inside of her chuba and placing it in the fire. When it began to burn, she used the hot wool to cauterize the wound and stop the bleeding. Dechen felt proud of her mother's resourcefulness.

The narrow cliff path the guide suggested was covered in deep snow and the group determined it was impassable. The only alternative was to go through the army camp below. The guide was dead-set against this choice. Saying he didn't want to be thrown into prison, he refused to accompany them any further. The group discussed their predicament and one of the monks agreed to continue guiding the group to safety, though he didn't know the rest of the way very well. No one was quite sure where to go or what to do. Between all the members there was very little money left, and no food. Some had heard rumors that Nepal's army wouldn't return them to the Chinese, so maybe it was okay to go that way. Collectively, a decision was agreed upon: they would take a chance and go to the army camp for help. Barely a few steps into the compound, the weary travelers found themselves surrounded by men with guns. A man who spoke Tibetan demanded to know where they were going.

"India," someone replied.

Nodding his head, he replied, "Follow me." He proceeded to walk toward a building, indicating there was food and rest inside. Obediently, the Tibetans followed him. In the building they were given apples and boiled potatoes to eat, and were told they could stay.

The group was instructed to separate into different sides of the house, one for men and one for women. Then the soldiers left and locked the doors from the outside. Lured by food and rest, they had become prisoners. For the next month, the Tibetans were held captive in the compound and forced into labor. Each day, they were taken up the mountain to chop trees and bring wood to the army compound. At night, they were locked into the building, not allowed to leave even to go to the bathroom. One night, a soldier came into the women's side of the building and, holding a gun to her head, tried to rape one of the women. The noise woke Tsering and another woman, and they scrambled to the defense. They pulled and pushed at the man, yelling and hitting him. They created such a ruckus that the men in the other area of the house heard the noises and ran to the aid of the women. The soldier tried to fight back but was outnumbered by the Tibetans. It became an all-out brawl, with Tsering leading the onslaught. Despite having a gun, the man realized he was defeated and retreated, locking the door behind him.

Given the time frame of Tsering and Dechen's journey, it's very likely that the soldiers were Maoist guerilla insurgents, not Nepali soldiers. The Tibetan captives, though providing free labor, ended up being a drain on the soldiers' minimal food resources—plus, they were a bit of an unruly bunch. In exchange for the Tibetans' freedom, the soldiers demanded money, threatening to send them back to the Chinese if they were not willing to pay. Agreeing that they'd suffered too much and come such a long way to be handed over to the Chinese, the Tibetans reluctantly combined some of what little money they had. Once the soldiers had been paid, they began releasing a few people every day. When it was their turn to leave, Dechen, her mother, a woman named Pema, and a monk named Gyatso were taken to an airport. As they made their way through the airport, Tsering noticed that Pema was no longer with them, and then saw the soldiers taking Pema out of the building by her arms. Tsering stormed over to them, insisting that they release Pema, but the men refused; they wanted to keep her with them. Loudly, so all around could hear her, Tsering declared, "Fine, then no one will go; we will all stay." She motioned for the monk and Dechen to come back to her. Glaring at the men in defiance, she pulled Pema away from the soldiers, making a loud scene as they moved past security and toward the airplane. Tsering had raised such a commotion that the men left hurriedly to avoid further scrutiny.

Dechen had no idea what to expect in this newest mode of transport. She had never seen an airplane up close, and was understandably excited and terrified. As the plane rumbled down the runway, she scooted as close as possible to her mother, eyes wide with wonder. Tsering had no explanation for how this iron beast would lift them into the sky, where they would end up, or how it came to be that they were being flown to Kathmandu instead of being tossed out of the encampment to fend for themselves. They had put their trust in the hands of people who had confined them to labor and could only pray their destination would be a safe one. When she gathered the courage to look out of one of the small windows of the propeller plane, Dechen could see for miles in the distance, and below her the snow-covered mountains she and her mother had spent so many weeks crossing. Eventually, the droning engines lulled her into sleep and carried her to a new world in Kathmandu, and the beginning of a new life.

Like so many before her, Dechen found Kathmandu and the Tibetan Refugee Transit Center (TRTC) a wonder, and Kathmandu a world apart from anything she knew. The fact that there were children there for her to play with was a bonus, and she was able to gradually shift into a new reality.

A few months after reaching the TRTC, mother and daughter were bussed to India and eventually to Dharamsala, where a few days later they attended an audience with His Holiness the Fourteenth Dalai Lama. It would not be the last time Dechen and her mother would meet him. Eventually, Dechen was sent to attend the Tibetan Children's Village (TCV) school in Gopalpur, India. She was not happy about being away from her mother, but eventually settled in and enjoyed learning. For the next eight years, she stayed and studied at the TCV school, returning to Dharamsala to visit her mother on holidays. While her daughter attended school, Tsering spent time in pilgrimage, traveling throughout India to sacred Buddhist locations.

In 2006, Dechen was one of several Tibetan students selected to travel to Denver, Colorado to attend the Tenth Annual PeaceJam global conference. She was chosen not because of her grades, which she claimed were not particularly high, but through an interview that must have impressed the teachers enough to select her for this singular opportunity. Dechen, along with other TCV students, joined 3,000 students from around the world and Nobel Peace laureates who had developed PeaceJam to inspire young generations of peacemakers. Dechen was on another adventure, albeit one far tamer than wandering the Tibetan Plateau and journeying through the Himalayas.

When I met Dechen in 2008, she was running a tiny hair salon with a friend. She had gone to beauty school in Delhi to ensure a future source of income for herself and her mother. Our friendship started then and continues today. She didn't last long as a hairstylist and eventually ended up teaching the Tibetan language to Western students of Buddhism seeking to read scripture. She lived in a small cement room with her mother, who was suffering from bad knees and problems with her back. Because of her age and physical condition, Tsering received a small stipend from the Central Tibetan Administration (CTA) to help with basic expenses. The powerful, outspoken woman of Dechen's childhood spent most of her days sitting, reading scripture, performing kora around the Tsuglagkhang, and visiting with friends. Dechen was and still is a devoted daughter.

It was during my second visit to McLeodganj that Dechen and I solidified our friendship. We talked about her life in India, her mother's health, and what she wanted for her future. At that time, getting out of India was foremost in her mind; whether back to Tibet or somewhere abroad, she wanted to free herself from the perpetual state of limbo she had lived in for years. Dechen went to work everyday at the immersion school, tutoring Westerners from all over the world. I didn't ask, but I imagined that interacting with people who had the kind of freedom she longed for was somewhat demoralizing. Dechen was always quick with a laugh, yet stoic. I never saw her vulnerability. One day, as we were talking about life in exile, she told me, "It's like being in a zoo; people come from all over the world to look at the Tibetans living in India. I feel like I'm an animal in a cage sometimes." I confessed to her that I had been one of those people. On my first visit five years earlier, I too ogled the Tibetans; I had been so eager for the opportunity to meet a "real" Tibetan, but through her and many others I had figured out pretty quickly that life in India for Tibetans was demoralizing. Dechen said she never felt settled, or like making a permanent home in one of the cement blocks that serve as housing for Tibetans in India. She felt no sense of permanence there, just adrift, in a state of limbo. Impermanence... how very Buddhist—yet in this case unwelcome.

Through an Australian humanitarian program that is specific to Tibetans, Dechen, her husband, their two children, and her mother Tsering were selected to resettle in Australia. It was Tsering's life story that put them in the lottery for this opportunity. The change in Dechen and her mother's lives is almost impossible to comprehend: from Tsering's privation in labor camps, to a very rustic, pastoral, nomadic life on the Tibetan Plateau, to living in poverty as exiles in the developing nation of India, to a fully modernized Australian city. Yet Dechen and her mother have made this newest transition seamlessly. Dechen volunteers some of her time to teach the Tibetan language to young children through the local chapter of the Tibetan Association in her city. The program is devoted to teaching Tibetan children the language, music, and other cultural elements of Tibet. Both of Dechen's children are thriving in Australia. Tsering is receiving proper medical care and spends most of her days quietly reading scripture, interacting with her grandchildren, and resting. Dechen continues to care for her mother. She plans on applying for citizenship as soon as she qualifies to do so. As to the subject of returning to Tibet, she is uneasy about seeing the changes there. The militarization, the heavy surveillance, the overall repression of Tibetans; thinking about all of it leaves her feeling sad and angry.

TIBETAN RESISTANCE

Being from Kham, the eastern portion of Tibet, Dechen and Tsering had family members involved in the early Tibetan resistance to China's invasion. That Tibetans resisted, conducting acts of guerilla-style warfare against the invaders, is a part of Tibet's modern history that is not well known. It's a fascinating piece of Cold War intrigue involving the United States Central Intelligence Agency that unfortunately ended quite sadly for Tibetans.[2]

Long before the Chinese Communist Party (CCP) sent troops to Chamdo, Tibet's fight for its independence had begun. The Central Tibetan Administration (CTA) was actively pursuing assistance from India, the UK, and the USA even before the People's Liberation Army (PLA) marched across China in 1949. With no meaningful army—approximately 10,000 troops—to defend the nation, there was little hope and few resources to fight against China's large, modern army, and Tibet's leaders knew what was to come. The Tibetans didn't stand a chance against the PLA.

Historically the unofficial defenders of Tibet's territory, the residents in the eastern province of Kham began acts of rebellion very early on. When the PLA arrived, the Khampa warriors did what they had always done: fight. They may not have had much in the way of modern weapons, but they had three things the Chinese did not: they were experts in horsemanship and the mountainous region; they were physically adapted to withstand high altitudes and harsh conditions; and they had a fierce commitment to defend their villages, monasteries, religion, and freedom from interlopers. Men and women resisted the PLA for years, eventually gaining support from the CIA. Known as Chushi Gangdruk (Four Rivers, Six Ranges), a reference to the terrain of eastern Tibet, these men would be trained by the CIA and would fight valiantly for many years.

The idea that Communism would spread across the world, especially after the horrors of World War II, was foremost in the minds of many democratic world leaders, especially in the USA, where anti-Communist sentiment was prevalent. President Truman, and later President Eisenhower, took the position that the CIA could participate in covert operations designed to develop underground resistance movements curtailing the advancement of Communism beyond the USSR and China in particular. In National Security Council Directive 5412/2 3, a confidential order signed by President Eisenhower in 1955, the CIA was directed to, "Create and exploit troublesome problems for International Communism (IC) ... discredit the prestige and ideology of IC ... develop underground resistance and facilitate covert and guerilla operations." According to the US State Department, the primary objective of the CIA's program was to "impede and harass the Chinese Communists." Tibet and the volunteer resistance fighters perfectly fit the bill for this directive.[3]

Through discussions with Gyalo Thondup, the Dalai Lama's older brother, the CIA agreed that the Tibetan resistance was organized and steadfast enough to justify support. Six men were chosen for the initial training, to be conducted in 1957 in Saipan. Eventually, the training was moved to Camp Hale in Leadville, Colorado, where the high altitude, cold climate, and mountainous terrain provided an ideal training site for the Tibetan fighters. The men were trained in hand-to-hand combat, sabotage, sending and receiving Morse code using the RS-1 spy radio, parachuting from airplanes, and of course in how to use the arsenal of US-supplied weapons. Nicknamed "ST Shadow Circus," the operation was highly secretive, given the sensitive nature of Cold War relations with China.

Some of the Tibetans involved in the operation believed that US support meant Tibet could wrest control of its territory from China, to eventually return to life in an independent Tibet. They hoped that all the refugees who had streamed into India, Nepal, and Bhutan would be able return home and resume the lives they had lived prior to the invasion.

That was not to be. The Chushi Gangdruk fighters who had dedicated their lives to the freedom of their small nation provided the CIA with an opportunity to gain intelligence for the US government and annoy the Communists per the official directive. Chushi Gangdruk was a fly in the ointment, so to speak. There was never any reality to the hope that with the help of the powerful US government, Tibet's freedom could be won.

The reality of Tibet's unimportance to the world at large was clearly demonstrated in the early 1970s, when the Nixon administration began overtures with the CCP in an effort to soften the hardline Cold War stance.

Nixon's 1972 China visit signaled a turning point and a change in diplomatic relations with the former Republic of China (ROC), whose government fled to Taiwan after losing the Civil War to the Mao-led Communists. After twenty-five years of closed relations with the CCP, Nixon was prepared to recognize it as the legitimate government of China. In late 1971, the CCP had replaced the ROC as the official representative of China on the United Nations Security Council. By 1972, the US had agreed to stop CIA funding for Chushi Gangdruk, which had been fighting in various forms for over twenty years. Yet even after the withdrawal of CIA support, the men continued to fight from the mountains of Mustang, Nepal, forcing the Dalai Lama to send a recorded message pleading for them to lay down their weapons and give up fighting. Most did give up, though some were so despondent they killed themselves rather than live with the demoralization of defeat.

CHAPTER 5

CHINA IN TIBET

China's interest in Tibet was, and still is, largely explained by geopolitics. Mao Zedong and other Communist Party leaders were initially eager to spread Communist ideology throughout all of Asia in order to gain control of the territory. Tibet was the first domino in that plan. Tibet's closest neighbor, India, had until 1947 been ruled by Great Britain, viewed by China as an Imperialist nation of the worst kind—which was understandable given the actions of British forces in the Opium Wars of the mid-1800s, as well as the short-lived 1903 British incursion into Tibet, which resulted in the signing of the Lhasa Convention. This British incursion was part of the "Great Game," a program of moves aimed at curtailing a potential Russian infiltration of India by using Tibet as a military buffer. The Lhasa Convention gave the British trade concessions, established a protectorate relationship over Tibet's foreign affairs, and granted a British representative stationed in Lhasa. However, the Qing Empire of China rejected the treaty, and Britain agreed not to annex Tibet, as well as acknowledging China's authority over the Buddhist nation. From a geopolitical viewpoint, the fact that the British had so easily been able to enter Tibet and enact a treaty with Tibetan leaders was a historical reference point for the emerging CCP. To prevent further foreign interference, Tibet had to be secured once and for all.

Tibet's relations with India, the UK, and the United States—another nation China reviled as Imperialist—were a threat to China that could potentially thwart Communist control over Asia or, worse, leave China vulnerable to attack from inside Tibet. Thus, like the British in the early twentieth century, Mao was keen to seize the small nation and use it as a military buffer zone. With Tibet under his thumb and military outposts stationed along the nation's border with India, China's security would be assured. Additionally, the Communists believed they could turn the Dalai Lama to their thinking and use him to convince Buddhists throughout Asia to accept Communism. While China has been successful in turning Tibet into a militarized zone, the Dalai Lama was, and remains, beyond their control.

Tibet was also seen as a treasure trove of natural resources for what would become a growing nation. The Roof of the World had vast stores of untapped timber in the east—which now have been well plundered—as well as numerous minerals—copper, zinc, cobalt, and lithium, to name a few. But by far the most valuable was water. Referred to as the "Water Tower of Asia," Tibet's mountains feed robust river systems that provide a third of the world's water supply. Thus, the Himalayas of Tibet are a gold mine for a resource-hungry nation like China. There are currently sixty-eight hydroelectric dams in Tibet, which tap into high-altitude rivers and lakes to provide power to the 1.4 billion citizens of China. These are rivers that feed into the Brahmaputra, Indus, and Mekong, waters vital to 3 billion people beyond China's borders, all increasingly at risk of being over-resourced. But it doesn't stop there; in 2024, China announced it would build a new dam, three times larger than the Three Gorges Dam, currently the world's largest hydropower station. At a projected cost of US$137 billion, the megaproject will be the largest hydropower dam in the world, harnessing the power of the Yarlung Tsangpo River in the Tibet Autonomous Region. This powerful river system is predicted to generate 50,000 megawatts of energy, twice that of the Three Gorges. The Yarlung Tsangpo boasts some of the most pristine and unexplored wilderness in the world. The negative impact on those who live beyond China's borders and depend on Tibet's water system for survival could incite unrest in the future, and with a warming climate many populations downstream are already feeling the effects of a decreasing water supply.[1]

China's reasons for making it not only illegal for Tibetans to cross the Himalayas but difficult to leave the country at all have evolved over time.

Given that the USA and other nations spend enormous amounts of money preventing people from illegally crossing *into* their territories, it does seem odd that China spends similar resources preventing people from leaving. However, as an authoritarian government, China must maintain political control, which feeds into national unity and ultimately security and the stability of the CCP. Tibetan refugees are viewed as a threat to China's control over Tibet. Since 1949, China has maintained the narrative that Tibetans welcomed the takeover, and that it was the aristocratic-theocratic system that had caused suffering in Tibet. China claims to have brought its beleaguered brothers and sisters back to the Motherland to save them from Imperialist influences. The reality is that China has not to this day been successful in winning over the Tibetan people's loyalty. The relationship is an uneasy and inequitable one, with China using hard power to force Tibetans to accept their place within the Chinese nation. China fears that the image of a flow of Tibetans fleeing to India for political reasons, or seeking the blessing of the Dalai Lama, runs contrary to the narrative that Tibetans are happy under Chinese rule, which ultimately undermines the CCP's narrative. Tibet is a very touchy subject for China's leaders because Tibetans have never completely integrated into Chinese society, nor have they unilaterally.

Further annoying the CCP, Tibetans continue to excel in the soft power of their cultural image, which began well over 100 years ago. The mythos of Tibet as a Shangri-La with a non-violent, religious, peace-loving people overpowered by a brutal aggressor remains the dominant Western view of the nation and its people. Causing further consternation for China's leaders, Tibetans in exile have the freedom to criticize and protest China's policies concerning their homeland, and can speak openly about mistreatment, discrimination, and repression. Exiled Tibetans can call for the preservation of Tibet's culture and language, and for religious freedoms, as well as for the full independence of Tibet. All of this negates the CCP's carefully constructed narrative that Tibetans are prosperous and happy under China's rule, and is an embarrassment for a very sensitive authoritarian regime. For China, full control of Tibet, whether by punitive force or assimilation, is vital. In the eyes of the Chinese Communist Party, there is no alternative.

Within China's borders, even a whiff of condemnation of its leaders or the CCP in general unleashes militarized actions to quell any disturbance that threatens the stability of the country—especially separatist sentiment from Tibetans, and more recently Uyghurs. Dissidents are regularly jailed without justification or trial, or are simply disappeared. As in many Communist and authoritarian nations, the government controls news and information, resulting in citizens who are none the wiser for the most part, and thus more easily controlled. International support is sympathetic to the plight of Tibet, but no global power recognizes it as anything but part of China. Though some Western nations advocate for Tibet's autonomy and of course human rights, the freedom to practice religion, and the preservation of Tibet's language and culture, Western powers have agreed to the "One China" doctrine—that Tibet is part of China. Attempts to chastise China for human rights abuses are toothless, nothing more than a wagging finger.

Preventing Tibetans from leaving their homeland whether through the mountains, "illegally," or with permission is something that China has managed to accomplish with a multipronged approach in recent years. Since 2008, the number of Tibetans crossing the Himalayas has decreased to nearly zero. For decades, the annual reported average was between 2,500 and 3,000 individuals. In 2017, only eighty Tibetans arrived in India from Tibet; ten arrived in 2022; and forty Tibetans made the journey in 2023. In the last fifteen years, fewer than 2,500 Tibetans in total have left Tibet through the Himalayas into Nepal and on to India.[2]

The downward trend began in 2008 on the heels of a Tibetan uprising that started in Lhasa and spread throughout the plateau, resulting in a lockdown of the Tibet Autonomous Region (TAR) and a sharp increase in surveillance throughout Tibetan-dominated areas. After the riots in 2008, the government strengthened its control by installing surveillance cameras throughout Tibetan-dominated cities, further deterring Tibetans' attempts to leave the country. The iron fist clenched even harder when a spate of self-immolations began in the eastern region of Sichuan—known as Kham to Tibetans—the first in 2009,[3] and then from 2011 continuing at an alarming pace for the next few years. As of this writing, a total of 160 Tibetans have self-immolated in acts of protest. Initially, monks carried out these acts, but eventually many nuns and lay people also participated. Through letters and the distribution of pamphlets, and through slogans shouted before and during lighting themselves on fire, they called for Tibetan independence, the return of the Dalai Lama to Tibet, and greater religious and cultural freedoms.

Rather than acknowledging the long-standing discontent and years of repression of the Tibetan people, or even attempting to understand what would cause such severe acts of protest, the CCP instead accused the Dalai Lama of instigating the acts. Family members were accused of inciting and or assisting in self-immolation, and grieving families were subjected to harsh punishments, including prison. Entire communities were locked down, internet and cell services were cut, and monks were imprisoned in their monasteries and forced to undergo re-education campaigns. Labeling the self-immolators as terrorists and criminals, the Chinese government deployed a heavy military presence in areas prone to protests. China's surveillance and heavy-handed militaristic approach to governance has been a strong deterrent to Tibetans wishing to secretly leave the country.

Additionally, China has steadily fortified political relations with neighboring Nepal via financial investments, including into the Nepali military, which has been used to increase border security, creating what is now one of the most heavily policed borders in the world. Not only can China easily monitor Tibetans in Nepal and along its borders, but it can also keep tabs on commonly used routes into Nepal from Tibet, which now sport surveillance cameras, guard towers, and fencing.[4] Nepal has come to rely on China's financial investments and complies with China's wish that it should arrest or deport fleeing Tibetans rather than allow them passage to India. Like the punishments for the families and communities of self-immolators, punishments for the families of escapees include job loss, forced relocation, or restricted movement. Escapees who are caught can face long prison sentences, torture, and of course China's forced patriotic re-education.

To further prevent Tibetans from leaving the country, minorities who wish to travel outside of China legally are up against a system that is clearly designed to discourage or prevent leaving altogether. With a two-tiered travel system that favors ethnic Chinese (Han), who can apply for and receive a passport in a relatively simple manner, Tibetans and other minority populations are at a distinct disadvantage. China's minority citizens are required to supply a large amount of documentation to apply for a passport and experience delays of up to five years, whereas the requirement for issuing Han Chinese citizens passports is fifteen days. This "fast-track/slow-track" system seems to be aimed primarily at those with religious affiliations—Hui Muslims, Tibetan Buddhists, and Uyghurs—who are often prevented from engaging in religious travel.

However, in late 2011, approximately 7,000 Tibetans were issued passports to attend the Dalai Lama's Kalachakra teachings in India. From Tibet they traveled to Nepal, and then on to India. Upon their return to Tibet, thousands were detained by the Chinese authorities, who claimed that the travel to India to attend teachings constituted splittist activities. Even though the detainees had received official passports to specifically attend the teachings, they were sent to a variety of detention facilities and were forced to undergo patriotic re-education for up to three months. Many of these Tibetans were elderly. It is important to note that of the 700 Han Chinese who also attended the teachings, no evidence was found that they also were detained upon their return. In 2012, restrictions were introduced in the TAR specifically linked to religious-oriented travel. These restrictions consider attending religious activities abroad as subversive political activity. Research by Human Rights Watch (HRW) finds that, "China's passport system in the TAR falls far short of international standards protecting the right to freedom of movement. The regulations are designed in a manner that discriminates on the basis of religion or ethnicity."[5]

Designed to further restrict travel, in 2012, TAR authorities also recalled all physical passports when the Chinese government began a nationwide conversion to ePassports. All TAR residents were required to hand in their passports, even if they were still current, ostensibly to be replaced by the new technology. Reports from HRW find, however, that ePassports were never issued to replace the confiscated and/or canceled regular passports for Tibetans living in the TAR.

Aside from the increased policing of borders, additional reasons that Tibetans are increasingly staying in Tibet may be related to some degree of assimilation among younger populations. Since China's occupation, Tibetans have been continuously exposed to the Chinese language, culture and music, and the dominant narrative that China—the great and benevolent nation—rescued Tibetans from a life of poverty and subservience to the Dalai Lama and his government. The narrative claims that Tibetans were always part of China's many ethnic minorities and never constituted an independent nation.

To succeed in assimilation, China is bent on the systematic erasure of Tibetan culture. One alarming method being used is forced assimilation of Tibetan children.[6] In the same way in which the USA, Canada, and Australia forced assimilation of indigenous people by rounding up children and putting them in boarding schools—a part of history for which all three nations have apologized in recent years due to the grievous harm the systems caused—China is using the boarding school method to erase Tibetan culture and create Mandarin-speaking citizens loyal to the Communist Party. Tibetan children have very little time at home with their families to learn the Tibetan way of life, customs, religion, language, and arts. In school, they are taught the Chinese account of Tibet's history and in far too many cases are unaware of additional perspectives. They become Chinese patriots, fluent in Mandarin rather than Tibetan. These are not children who when reaching adulthood will have an intense interest in crossing the Himalayas to see His Holiness the Fourteenth Dalai Lama, a man whom some do not even know exists. There is a slow and intentional erasure of Tibetan identity, except when it is carefully curated specifically for the purposes of tourism, entertainment, and as a show presented to the outside world and to Chinese citizens that all is well in Tibet.[7]

Combined, these three prongs are gradually producing the result China wants: a subjugated minority culture that can be controlled to avert CCP humiliation, decrease resistance, and ultimately bring Tibetans into line with China's overall One China policy. Whether it will work in full remains to be seen. Even under a totalitarian regime of repression, the hope is that Tibetans will not forget who they are, what they were, and that, ultimately, they are a subjugated populace in their own country.

CHAPTER 6

LIFE IN EXILE

Millions worldwide live as refugees in a perpetual state of uncertainty, unable to return home or having witnessed their homelands reduced to rubble. Tibetans in exile understand this reality acutely, having endured the profound loss of home, family, and displacement from the land of their birth and of their ancestors. Even Tibetans born in India experience a poignant sense of deprivation, their identity intrinsically linked to a land they have never intimately known. Statelessness, the lack of citizenship, traps individuals in this limbo, raising the question of how to forge a meaningful life amid such conditions. The collective trauma stemming from this powerlessness is undeniable. While the yearning to return to Tibet persists, to do so demands sacrificing fundamental freedoms and accepting constant surveillance and marginalization. Consequently, many Tibetans seek citizenship in democratic nations with better economic opportunities, aiming eventually to return as visitors to the land of their ancestors, mitigating the pain of separation.

In McLeodganj and other Tibetan settlements in India and Nepal, as well as in North America, Europe, and wherever Tibetans are living outside of Tibet, the overt politics of Tibet and China are ever-present, as are the more subtle qualities of a life lived with the burdens and inequities of displacement. Within the exiled community in India, there are two types of Tibetans: those who were born in Tibet, lived part of their lives there, and then escaped to India; and those who were either born in India or are too young to remember life in Tibet. The latter have been schooled in India from birth or a very young age and are first-generation exiles; they or their parents have built businesses, and many speak Hindi fluently, yet because of the strength of the exiled community they have for the most part resisted assimilation into their host's culture. They are not Indian; they are not Chinese; they are tsampa eaters, Tibetan through and through, just like Tibetans who grew up or spent the formative years of their lives in Tibet and later crossed the mountains into India. The difference between them comes down to lived experience. Few of those born and raised in India or Nepal have seen Tibet outside of pictures or videos. They've heard stories about life in Tibet but have not lived it—unlike the *newcomers*, who were raised in Tibet and carry memories and actual photos of life in Phayul (Fatherland) and still have family living there. The yearning and ache for home are slightly different for those who were too young to remember or were born and raised outside of Tibet. Cheated out of something that is rightfully theirs, they cannot attain it; they do not carry pictures of Tibet in their memory or pockets because they've never been there, yet the yearning is as persistent and maybe more so than among their Tibet-born counterparts. In "*My Tibetanness*," activist and writer Tenzin Tsundue, born in India, expresses this frustration and sense of loss he and other Tibetans born outside of Tibet feel.

I am Tibetan.
I am not from Tibet.
Never been there.
Yet I dream
of dying there.

For Tibetans born in India or Nepal, the likelihood of walking in the land of their ancestors is slim at best. In 2011, Tibetan artist Tenzing Rigdol smuggled twenty-two tons of Tibetan soil into Dharamsala. The installation brought hundreds of Tibetans, who touched, smelled, tasted, and walked upon the soil as if it were the most sacred act imaginable. The risks taken to bring soil from Tibet across the border exemplify the lengths to which many will go to reach home.

In reverse, it's essential to consider the unique relationship Tibetans have with His Holiness the Dalai Lama, one that drives so many to leave the comfort of home to cross the Himalayas from Tibet into Nepal and India. While Tibetans born and raised in India have lived near His Holiness all their lives, those raised in Tibet were deprived. They risk a death-defying journey, leaving family and home behind to meet a man who represents to them the heart of their beloved Tibet and their Buddhist faith. To make a pilgrimage to the Dalai Lama, regardless of the effort or sacrifice, is of monumental importance. The manner in which the Dalai Lama resides in the collective and individual psyche of many Tibetans is partially the result of seven centuries of tradition, but more likely is a direct result of that tradition nearly being destroyed by China's occupation and continued colonization of Tibet. The Dalai Lama is not allowed to visit Tibet; in fact, he has been exiled from Tibet since his departure on March 17, 1959. Even though he still lives and teaches, his former homes, the Potala Palace and the Norbulingka, are now tourist attractions.

Intermingled with age-old superstitious beliefs and the enormous influence of the Tibetan version of Buddhism, packed with its mystery and elaborate ritual, the Dalai Lama is not merely a religious and temporal leader but is considered by many to be the heart and soul of Tibetan culture.

Born in the small village of Takster in Tibet's Amdo Province in 1935, Lhamo Thondup lived with his family in a typical rural Tibetan home, constructed of rammed-earth walls, wood beams, and hardened-earth floors, with no electricity or running water. He was identified at the age of two as the reincarnation of the former Thirteenth Dalai Lama through premonitions, an elaborate search, and a series of specific tests designed to prove he was indeed the Fourteenth Dalai Lama. Thus began a life of monasticism, spiritual training, enormous responsibility, and great privilege, all in preparation to lead the small nation. When in 1949 the Chinese Communist Party succeeded in overthrowing the Chinese Nationalist Party, which fled to Taiwan, it was clear to the Tibetan government that the Communists would quickly turn their attention to Tibet as the first step to expand their reach throughout Asia. This forced the fifteen-year-old Dalai Lama to accept his temporal duties three years earlier than normal. Thrust into the political sphere, he would learn to contend with leaders far more experienced than he was. The belief that his consciousness had lived thirteen prior lives as the Dalai Lama of Tibet was supposed to have given him the confidence to know what steps to take. He has lived an extraordinary life, one beset by immense challenges from a very tender age that encumbered the young boy with an unwinnable situation that was to play out on the world's stage during the Cold War, and which continues to this day.

PRESERVING TIBETAN CULTURE

During their time in exile, Tibetans have put their energy to good use by capturing the experiences and histories of those who lived through the Chinese invasion and occupation. Rather than lose those memories to time, the early years of violence, land reforms, destruction of monasteries, labor camps, starvation, and hundreds of thousands of deaths have been preserved meticulously in exile. In addition to recording lived experiences, the exiled population, with the leadership of His Holiness the Fourteenth Dalai Lama and the Central Tibetan Administration (CTA), have put remarkable effort into preserving the Tibetan culture in a holistic manner, from a functioning government system that spans the globe, to a comprehensive educational system, and a variety of efforts to preserve Tibetan culture outside of Tibet.

Due to China's policies and efforts to restrict travel, it's noteworthy that the broader Tibetan exile population in India has been experiencing a decline. In part, the decline is attributed to factors such as migration to Western countries, but there is also a reduced influx from Tibet due to China's policies and schemes to prevent Tibetans leaving the country. This trend is concerning as it influences the demographic composition of Tibetan communities in areas like McLeodganj and the other settlements in India, which in turn could negatively impact the government systems the CTA has created. Today, those systems of governance are firmly in place, well organized, and will continue unabated for the foreseeable future.

THE CENTRAL TIBETAN ADMINISTRATION

The Dalai Lama officially established the Central Tibetan Administration (CTA) from his exile in northern India in late April 1959, as a continuation of the government that had escaped from Tibet. Set up as a democracy, the CTA was developed to not only govern the exiled population, but also in preparation for a return to Tibet. In the beginning, it was believed that Tibet would gain its freedom and Tibetans would return home. However, it was not long before it became clear that Tibet's freedom would not happen overnight, if at all. The CTA in exile was set up with the idea that if and when Tibet's independence was achieved, the exiled government would be dissolved and a transitional government led by Tibetans currently residing in Tibet would establish a democracy. That is still the position today. The CTA is funded primarily from private donations; the USA and India contribute annually to the CTA and a small amount of revenue is received from exiled Tibetans. The exiled government is very well organized and officially run mainly from offices in lower Dharamsala and from Tibetan bureaus in Paris, Brussels, Amsterdam, Berlin, New Delhi, New York, and Washington, DC.

The CTA consists of departments one would typically find in a nation: Health, Education, Security, Finance, Information, International Relations, Culture, and, of course, Religion. The government is overseen by the Kalon Tripa, or Sikyong—essentially an elected prime minister—a cabinet known as the Kashag, and a parliament consisting of members who live in India, North America, Europe, and Australia. Each member of parliament represents one of the four branches of Tibetan Buddhism—Kagyu, Nyingma, Sakya, and Gelug—and the ancient pre-Buddhist Bön religion, and the three original provinces of Tibet: Kham (Do-toe), Amdo (Domey), and Ü-Tsang. The CTA is guided by a charter influenced by the UN's Universal Declaration of Human Rights that guarantees for all Tibetans "equality before the law and enjoyment of rights and freedom without discrimination on the basis of sex, religion, race, language and social origin." Additionally, the charter guarantees a separation of powers between the legislature, judiciary, and executive branches of government. Traditionally the head of the Tibetan government, in 2011, the Fourteenth Dalai Lama dissolved his political authority to the elected Sikyong as part of furthering a democratic system.[1] It was also likely a move to thwart any political control China might attempt to wield by choosing the next Dalai Lama.

EDUCATION IN EXILE

When the young Dalai Lama first settled in Dharamsala after his escape in 1959, he was faced with the problem of what to do with the many children who over the subsequent years had made the trek with parents or relatives escaping Tibet. It quickly became imperative to care for not only the adults who had been displaced, and in many cases were ill and destitute, but also the children, many of whom had been orphaned when parents had succumbed either during the trek through the mountains or to a variety of illnesses after reaching India. From humble beginnings as a nursery for just over fifty malnourished and ill children, the Tibetan Children's Village (TCV) has become a success story among Tibet's exiled population in India. Under the direction of the Dalai Lama, the small makeshift nursery grew to a full-time boarding school. In 1964, the Dalai Lama convinced his younger sister Jetsun Dechen to take over the direction of the school, and she served as its president for forty-two years. As more children arrived in India, the schools were expanded to branches in other locations. Currently, the K-12 schools range from the northernmost part of India, in Ladakh, to as far south as Bylakyppe, caring for and educating nearly 17,000 students across the TCV's eight residential branches.

The residential TCVs operate in the fashion of a traditional boarding school, providing housing, food, and education, but in a unique twist also provide parenting. Students are grouped by age and school year and are assigned a home mother and sometimes a home father who act as parents for each group. These groups and their parents stay together as the children make their way through the K-12 system. Because children are living away from their birth families or are orphaned, a family is created so that they feel loved, supported, and safe throughout the education process.

The curriculum is comprehensive, including English and the Tibetan language, math, science, art, and music, as well physical exercise. The Tibetan culture and religion run through much of the education students receive, which is guided by the motto: "Others Before Self. Come to Learn, Go to Serve." The goals of the TCV say much about the Tibetan culture and its core beliefs. The school's traditional education, though rigorous, is anchored by values that make the system so unique. TCV states the goals of the education system as to: provide parental care and love; develop a sound understanding of Tibetan identity and culture; develop character and moral values; provide effective modern and Tibetan education; provide a child-centered learning atmosphere in the schools; provide an environment for physical and intellectual growth; provide a suitable and effective life and career guidance for social and citizenship skills.

The network of TCV schools includes eight residential schools, three day schools for younger children living with their parents, three vocational and industrial training schools, higher-education assistance, three youth hostels for students attending college in India, and the Dalai Lama Institute for Higher Education.

The CTA established a Department of Education in 1960 to ensure the education of refugees and eventually Tibetans born in exile. The department has grown over the years to include four main branches, the Sambhota Tibetan Schools Society, the Snow Lion Foundation, the Tibetan Homes Foundation (providing care for the elderly), and TCV. In all, there are sixty-two schools in India and Nepal providing education and care for Tibetan students.

PRESERVING HISTORY AND CULTURE

Through the Tibet Oral History Project and comprehensive history books, Tibetans and Western allies have diligently recorded the details of Tibet's history from the Tibetans who lived through the early years of invasion and occupation, by capturing their direct experiences.[2] The Library of Tibetan works and Archives in lower Dharamsala conserves Tibetan manuscripts, books, artifacts, and works of art, and provides opportunities for research and Tibetan language classes. Documenting Tibet's history is vital in the face of the CCP's adherence to the revisionist narrative it has created.

As well as history, the CTA and the exiled population of Tibetans devote much effort to the preservation of their overall heritage. In McLeodganj, the Tibetan Institute of Performing Arts (TIPA) trains young Tibetan performers in traditional Tibetan music and dance. Performing around the world since 1975, TIPA musicians and dancers showcase an important element of Tibet's heritage, music, opera, singing, instruments, and of course dancing in traditional costumes. Another organization helping to preserve Tibetan culture is the serene and beautiful Norbulingka Institute, a short drive from Dharamsala. The institute's masters have been training Tibetan students in traditional craftsmanship since 1995. At the institute, students live, work, and learn all modalities of Tibetan art and craftsmanship. The exquisite results of their handiwork are sold locally and internationally. In addition, wherever Tibetans live outside of India and Tibet, Tibetan associations are formed, designed to preserve the rich culture, provide community, educate Tibetan children, and advocate for the Tibetan cause. Within these associations, young Tibetan children regularly attend Sunday school, where they learn the Tibetan language, music, dance, and their cultural traditions. The associations also provide opportunities for Tibetans to gather for community activities, protests, prayer vigils, and to host dignitaries from the Tibetan government in exile.

Despite the concerted effort to keep the heritage and culture of Tibet alive outside of their homeland, assimilation occurs among Tibetan exiles whether in India, the USA, Europe, or other Western nations, and more so with second and third generations. The dissolution of cultural heritage is happening regardless of the important attempts to save it, making the threat to Tibetan culture and language a chilling reality, so these preservation methods are vital and will be key to keeping the Tibetan culture and language alive.

Life in Exile

TIBETAN INDEPENDENCE

By the mid-1980s, fully understanding the realities of global politics and the intractable conflict he found himself facing, the Dalai Lama shifted his approach to Tibet's independence altogether. After much consultation, he abandoned Tibet's cause for full independence and instead adopted the Middle Way Approach and the Five Point Peace Plan.[3] In brief, the approach agrees that Tibet will remain part of China and not seek independence, and the Five Point Peace Plan lays out what that should entail. In the plan, Tibet would become a zone of peace: military activity would cease; the transfer of Chinese into Tibetan areas would cease; Tibetan human rights would be respected and Tibetans would have democratic freedom; Tibet's pristine environment would be restored and protected, with nuclear weapons abandoned and waste dumping to cease; and negotiations between Tibet and China on the future status of Tibet would continue.

Thus far, China has remained steadfastly disinterested in earnest conversations with Tibetans on these five points, or any other topics. This is understandable, as in essence what's being asked for is for all three Tibetan-recognized provinces—Kham, Amdo, and Ü-Tsang—to be self governed by Tibetans within the borders of China, a proposition that runs contrary to the way in which the Chinese government operates. While there are autonomous regions in Tibetan areas, the idea that they would have democratic freedom is preposterous from the standpoint of the CCP. Making the three provinces of Tibet a zone of peace would completely dismantle the militarized buffer zone that China has established between itself and India. The Five Point Peace Plan is a noble idea and might work if one were dealing with an adversary that could comprehend that making peace with Tibetans and allowing a degree of liberty would alleviate the need for the immense effort China exerts in maintaining security over the restive region.

Although it was made with the support of some of the exiled population, instituting the Middle Way Approach meant that reclaiming Tibet as a fully self-governing independent nation was no longer a pursuit of the exiled leader and the CTA. And while Tibetans do not want to go against His Holiness out of a deep respect for him, many do not to this day agree with this approach. Feeling that the Dalai Lama has capitulated to the Chinese, many are willing to voice their discontent. Organizations like Students for a Free Tibet (SFFT), The Tibetan Youth Congress (TYC), and the Rangzen Alliance support an independent Tibet to varying degrees. They straddle a precarious line between respecting their beloved spiritual leader and disagreeing with him completely. Those that support the Middle Way Approach feel that Tibetans who don't are insulting His Holiness, and this has led to a growing discord among the exiled population. The choice to follow either the Dalai Lama's Middle Way Approach for Tibet or full independence from China has resulted in a fractured message from Tibetans in exile. The Dalai Lama on the one hand insists he is not a splittist—an oft-repeated accusation from the Chinese—and accepts that Tibet is part of China, and on the other hand Tibetans in exile and many in Tibet protest, regularly calling for Tibet's freedom from Chinese rule. How could the CCP believe the Dalai Lama, with these two dichotomies playing out side by side? Protests in Tibet just add fuel to the fire, making the situation intractable.

CONCLUSION

Seventy-five years have passed since China's People's Liberation Army (PLA) set foot in Chamdo, Tibet on October 7, 1950, starting an occupation that China currently enjoys without challenge from outside forces. Much has changed in Tibet over the past eight decades; but Tibetans are no freer inside Tibet today than they were when the Chinese Communist Party (CCP) first began taking control of the nation. China's government has worked tirelessly to revise Tibet's history before and after Communist control and continues to whitewash any event involving Tibetans that does not align with the carefully crafted, though transparently outlandish, accounting of Tibetan life in Tibet—that Tibetans are better off than they were under the Dalai Lama's governance, more prosperous, and better educated. It's true that Tibetans have had better access to education and financially have more money than many had seventy-five years ago. However, there is a fiscal disparity between higher-earning Han Chinese and their Tibetan counterparts, who earn significantly less. Tibetans' access to education in the last two decades has increased, but at the cost of losing Tibetan language in that education and feeling the sting of disparity driven by racism. The result of China's governance is the marginalization of Tibetans in their own country.

China's control of Tibet has not yielded the results it initially intended. Overall, the policies China has put in place have been a miscalculation. Its roughshod treatment of the Tibetan people, and its lack of respect for the unique Tibetan culture and the vital component religion plays in the lives of Tibetans, has revealed that a heavy-handed approach to ethnic minorities in China is not sustainable. Because of its insensitivity, China has faced continued criticism for human rights violations, claims of cultural genocide, and the destruction of Tibet's once-pristine environment. The Chinese government is incredibly sensitive to any criticism of its handling of Tibet or the Tibetan people; it's sensitive about criticism of any kind, but Tibet is an area of particular sensitivity, and one China refuses to compromise on.

Under intense repression from the Chinese government, the Tibetan people continue to straddle the precarious line between self-preservation and speaking the truth at their peril. In general, the Tibetan people are not happy with their lives under China's rule, as is evident from the uprisings and various forms of protest that continue even into the eighth decade. The CCP's refusal to engage with the Tibetan exiled government in meaningful negotiations, continued diatribes against His Holiness the Dalai Lama, and militaristic response to Tibetan discontent throughout the plateau have ultimately revealed a weakness in the CCP. Heightened repression, surveillance, and a continued military presence in Tibetan areas is a sign of China's desperation to wrest control of a people that continue to resist assimilation, and may never yield the results China desires. Thus, the CCP will continue to spend enormous energy and money trying to tame Tibet with militaristic force, and it will continue to lose.

The approach China's Communist Party leaders have taken in Tibet has been mostly unsuccessful. They have historically lacked respect for Tibet's culture and the fact that religion is the very backbone of Tibetan society. Instead, the CCP has sought to repress and destroy religious institutions, even going so far as to install police and surveillance in monasteries to prevent monks from leading or inciting protests.

Another approach China has taken involves the recognition of reincarnated spiritual leaders. Prior to the Dalai Lama's ninetieth birthday celebration in 2025, he confirmed that upon his death he will reincarnate in a free country and that the Gaden Phodrang Trust has sole authority for locating his successor. He noted, "No one else has any authority." This was a clear message to the world that China's involvement should not be seen as legitimate. China shot back immediately: "The Chinese government upholds the principle of independence and self-governance in religious affairs and administers the reincarnation of Living Buddhas, including that of the Dalai Lama, in accordance with the law. No interference by any external forces will be allowed."[1] China's intent is of course to control Tibetan Buddhism inside Tibet by installing a puppet political leader, much as it did with the Eleventh Panchen Lama, a move that was unsuccessful. The story of the Eleventh Panchen Lama is considered tragic among Tibetans, and annual vigils have been held since the young boy's disappearance. In 1989, upon the death of the Tenth Panchen Lama, in keeping with the Tibetan tradition, the Dalai Lama was responsible for locating and naming his successor. However, China insisted that it had the authority to make that selection. What ensued was a power struggle between China and the Dalai Lama. In 1995, the Dalai Lama recognized six-year-old Gedhun Choekyi Nyima as the Eleventh Panchen Lama. Three days later, he was abducted from his home in Tibet and disappeared along with his family. Their whereabouts remain unknown.[2]

Contrary to the methods Tibetans have used for centuries, the Chinese made their own choice and named a different Panchen Lama, who has since failed to be recognized by anyone in or outside of Tibet as anything other than the Panchen zuma ("false Panchen"). Choosing influential Tibetan Buddhist incarnations is another of China's desperate ploys to gain control over the Tibetan populace. It didn't work with the Panchen Lama, and it most definitely won't work with the Dalai Lama. It is yet another example of the continued failure of the Chinese government to understand and respect Tibetan culture, and hence why unrest in Tibet will continue for the foreseeable future.

More recently, the tack China has taken is to "Chinafy" Tibetan Buddhism with the help of the "false Panchen." This translates to removing the elements of Tibetan Buddhism that make it so unique, elements that evolved over time on the Roof of the World, influenced by the intense seclusion of the vast and wild Tibetan Plateau as it was hundreds of years ago, and by the high mountains, rugged terrain, and pre-modern society. While Tibetan Buddhism incorporates all the elements of the Buddhist teaching it received from India—the birthplace of Buddhism—in the isolation and deep silence of the mountainous country, the religion took on a patina of grand ritual, bold color, mystery, and a plethora of gods and goddesses akin to Hinduism. The religion is a reflection of the Tibetan people and the land they have inhabited for thousands of years. For the Chinese government to erase that unique evolution of Tibetan Buddhism would be yet another tragedy for Tibetan culture.

Possibly the largest mistake China has made is in restricting access to the Fourteenth Dalai Lama. If it expected that with his absence from Tibet his people would forget about him, it was wrong. Being out of reach to the Tibetan people has made him even more important, more popular, and ultimately a more powerful influence in the minds of Tibetans, regardless of where they live. The Dalai Lama's global status as a man of peace and compassion has given him an enormous platform as the ambassador of the Tibetan people and of Buddhism. He has won the hearts and minds of millions of people the world over, making him an incredibly annoying thorn in China's side. His message of love and compassion is a far more effective tool than the repression, violence, and surveillance China metes out. Had China chosen to make amends early on and allowed the Dalai Lama to visit Tibet unrestricted and safe, this alone would have gone a long way to preventing years of unrest.

China is playing the long game on Tibet: that, given enough time, Tibetans will forget the past, stop resisting, and accept their place within the fabric of China's nation-state. Were they to become more Chinese than Tibetan, China's leaders would be pleased no end. Indoctrinating Tibetan children in boarding schools is part of that long-term goal; if Western history is any indicator of how that worked out, China will fail at that plan as well. They also believe that choosing the reincarnated Lamas, including the next Dalai Lama, will provide them the control over the Tibetan populace they seek. But since they failed to capture the hearts and minds of Tibetans with their choice of the Panchen Lama, choosing the next Dalai Lama would be even worse, an egregious and unforgiveable mistake.

If China wishes to see calm and quiet in Tibet, the simple solution is to allow full autonomy to all three historical regions of Tibet, and to maintain good relations with India, Nepal, and Bhutan, thus eliminating the need for a militarized zone completely. Most importantly, allowing the Dalai Lama to visit all of Tibet without restriction would go far in quelling the discontent among the Tibetan population. However, it is in the nature of the Chinese government to save face at all costs, rather than being subjected to the humiliation of admitting it's been wrong about Tibet in every way possible.

In the imagination of the Western world, Tibet continues to wield a mythical quality that garners support from political leaders and everyday citizens—and the same is true even among some Buddhist Chinese citizens. This soft power is one of Tibet's greatest assets, one that has lasted for well over a century. Though support is emotional rather than practicable, it continues to keep the flame of Tibet alive as a unique place and culture. The death of the Fourteenth Dalai Lama will very likely be a cataclysmic event inside of Tibet. How the Chinese respond to the swell of unrest that is sure to occur will be, no doubt, violent and tragic.

If the Fourteenth Dalai Lama lives to 110 or 140 years of age, as he professes, maybe a tragedy could be avoided. This is, of course, a long shot. What the long-range future for Tibet holds is unknowable. There's no indication that the current leadership in China will change course. In fact, Xi Jinping has been more of a hardliner than was originally expected.

Currently, the spirit of the Tibetan people remains alive in Tibet and is thriving in exile. The work of the exiled population is keeping that spirit and devotion to their culture and religion steadfast on behalf of their brothers and sisters living under the rule of China's occupation.

As for Dechen, Lhamo, Dolma, and Bhuti, though living far from Tibet, their Tibetan identity is as strong as ever. Tsampa eaters all.

NOTES

NOTES TO THE INTRODUCTION

1. Tibetans with the opportunity to emigrate to a Western nation look forward to the day they can become citizens so that they can legally travel back to Tibet.

NOTES TO CHAPTER 1: BULLETS IN THE SNOW

1. Over the course of thousands of years, Tibetans have developed genetic traits that include relatively low hemoglobin levels, more efficient ventilation, better cardiopulmonary function, and better reproductive viability at high altitude.

2. Climbers who witnessed the shooting reported that even after being shot, Ani Kelsang pulled herself forward along the ground off and on for some time.

3. The Tibetan Refugee Transit Center in Kathmandu is partially funded by the United Nations High Commissioner for Refugees (UNHCR), with the Central Tibetan Administration mainly responsible for operating the center in accordance with UN policy. The UNHCR helps to ensure that refugees are treated for medical issues, and are protected until they reach their destination, in this case India.

4. US Customs and Border Protection, "Border Patrol Overview: Mission," January 5, 2011. Archived from the original on October 17, 2009. www.cbp.gov/border-security/along-us-borders/overview#:~:text=Border%20Patrol%20Operations,motorcycles%2C%20bicycles%2C%20and%20snowmobiles.

NOTES TO CHAPTER 2: ON THE RUN

1. Tibetan clothing is unique to Tibetans, much like that of Indigenous North American tribes or other peoples who have been marginalized. Cultural appropriation was my concern.

2. China Tibet Broadcasting (Tibet TV) is a state-run Tibetan-language station broadcasting throughout China and to India.

NOTES TO CHAPTER 3: SISTERS

1. Circling the base of Mt. Kailash begins at an altitude of 15,000 feet, climbing to 18,550 feet at about the halfway point. Many people break the trek up into three to four days, camping along the way. Tibetans often do it in one day. Climbing the mountain itself is not allowed due to the many religions that revere Mt. Kailash as sacred and who believe it is the earth's *axis mundi*—the point at which earth meets heaven.

NOTES TO CHAPTER 4: THE LONG PILGRIMAGE

1. Beginning in 1953, peasants were "encouraged" to join communes that collectivized farming and animal husbandry. Privately owned land was abolished. During the Great Leap Forward, People's Communes were developed to increase the production of food supplies—but were unsuccessful.

2. Excellent books on the subject include *Orphans of the Cold War: America and the Tibetan Struggle for Survival* by Kenneth Knaus (1999) and Carol McGranahan's *Arrested Histories: Tibet, the CIA, and Memories of a Forgotten War (2010)*.

3. Covert operations were a major part of the United States' geopolitical policy, especially during the Cold War. Secret and highly classified activities took place across the globe. Where Communism was concerned, the overall objective was to discredit the ideology in favor of democracy and ultimately capitalism. US Department of State, *National Security Council Directive NSC 5412/2, Covert Operations,* December 28, 1955. https://history.state.gov/historicaldocuments/frus1950-55Intel/d250.com.

NOTES TO CHAPTER 5: CHINA IN TIBET

1. Medog Hydropower Station was approved in December 2024. Dubbed "China's New Great Wall" by *The New York Times*, the completed project could have negative impacts on ecosystems, biodiversity, and the lives of locals and downstream neighbors. The Yarlung Tsangpo River is known as the Brahmaputra in India, and is a significant source of water for India and Bangladesh. Geopolitics are at play and tensions are high in the affected areas.

2. The number of Tibetans reaching India has decreased dramatically, leading to a decrease in the number of Tibetan exiles. There are concerns that the dwindling number of Tibetans in exile will have calamitous long-term effects on the ability of the Central Tibetan Administration to continue, as well as on monasteries and students in Tibetan-run schools. *Hindustan Times*, "Dharamshala's Tibetan Tide Ebbs, Arrivals Fall Steeply Amid China's Strict Border Vigil," August 19, 2024. www.hindustantimes.com/cities/chandigarh-news/dharamshalas-tibetan-tide-ebbs-arrivals-fall-steeply-amid-china-s-strict-border-vigil101723912921340.html.com.

3. The first known self-immolation and death in Tibet was by a young monk named Tapey from Kirti Monastery in 2009.

4. The Nepal–China border has been built up since 2008 to include concrete ramparts, fences, barbed wire, and guarded sentry towers. Hannah Beech and Bhadra Sharma, "China's 'New Great Wall' Casts a Shadow on Nepal'," *The New York Times*, October 12, 2024. www.nytimes.com/interactive/2024/10/12/world/asia/china-nepal-borders.html.

5. Human Rights Watch, "*China: End Two-Tier Travel System for Tibetans, Others. Passport Cancellations Used to Restrict Religious Minorities' Rights,*" July 13, 2015. www.hrw.org/news/2015/07/13/china-end-two-tier-travel-system-tibetans-others.

6. China's boarding school system was established in the 1950s to provide access to education in rural areas. In recent years, private village schools teaching in the Tibetan language have been closed and boarding schools have become the main form of education, spurring claims that China aims to erase or undermine the Tibetan identity beginning with the youngest members of society.

7. "Insensitive voyeurism" is a term that describes cultural traditions being marketed as tourist attractions. Some of the tourism is entwined with CCP propaganda that serves to legitimize China's presence in Tibet. For example, Chinese tourists have been dropped off by the busload to noisily watch, photograph, and film the deeply sacred sky burials. This level of disrespect strips the ancient Tibetan tradition of its dignity and its deeper religious significance.

NOTES TO CHAPTER 6: LIFE IN EXILE

1. Ending a 368-year-old tradition of past and future Dalai Lamas acting as temporal and spiritual heads of the Tibetan people and government, the Fourteenth Dalai Lama signed into law a formal transfer of temporal leadership to the Sikyong, elected democratically by the exiled Tibetan population.

2. The Tibetan Oral History Project was founded in 2003 by Marcella Adamski at the suggestion of the Fourteenth Dalai Lama. The project has collected 304 interviews with Tibetan elders who lived in an unoccupied Tibet, who have related the stories of their lives and experiences before and since China's occupation. See www.tibetoralhistory.org/.

3. The Five Point Peace Plan was introduced in 1987. Tenzin Gyatso, the Fourteenth Dalai Lama of Tibet, was awarded the Nobel Peace Prize in 1989 for the peaceful solution he developed to the Tibet–China conflict.

In 1988, the Dalai Lama proposed the Middle Way Approach for Tibet, offering coexistence between the Tibetan and Chinese people. The plan states in part: "The Tibetan people do not accept the present status of Tibet under the People's Republic of China. At the same time, they do not seek independence for Tibet, which is a historical fact. Treading a middle path in between these two lies the policy and means to achieve a genuine autonomy for all Tibetans living in the three traditional provinces of Tibet within the framework of the People's Republic of China." See www.dalailama.com/messages/tibet/middle-way-approach.

NOTES TO THE CONCLUSION

1. China's ambassador to India, Xu Feihong, as well as other Chinese foreign diplomats, immediately took to the news and social media to denounce the Dalai Lama's reincarnation plans. *The Economic Times*, "Dalai Lama's Reincarnation 'Inherently an Internal Affair of China,' Says Chinese Envoy," July 7, 2025. https://economictimes.indiatimes.com/news/international/world-news/dalai-lamas-reincarnation-inherently-an-internal-affair-of-china-says-chinese-envoy/articleshow/122283921.cms?from=mdr.

2. Born in China and recognized in 1995 by the Fourteenth Dalai Lama as the Eleventh Panchen Lama, six-year-old Gedhun Choekyi Nyima was abducted shortly after by the Chinese government. He and his family have not been seen in public since. The Chinese government failed to successfully put forward a substitute of its choosing because the Tibetan people would not accept him. It is believed that the CCP wanted to install its puppet Panchen Lama, as traditionally it is the Panchen Lama who chooses the next Dalai Lama. The UN, human rights organizations, and numerous nation-states have continued to call for the release of Choekyi Nyima.

ACKNOWLEDGMENTS

Many of the people I owe a debt of gratitude to I've never met in person, nor spoken to. But their work has been a tremendous guide in my Tibetan history education. Namely Tsering Shakya, Ph.D., Associate Professor at the University of British Columbia where he is the Canada Research Chair in Religion and Contemporary Society in Asia. Shakya is the author of *Dragon in the Land of Snows: A History of Modern Tibet Since 1947*, the first definitive accounting of Tibet's modern history, which provided the scaffolding from which I began my journey into understanding the intractable conflict between Tibet and China. In *Tibet: An Unfinished Story*, by Lezlee Brown Halper and Stefan Halper traverses the same territory as Shakya with newer declassified documents and places a focus on the geopolitical underpinnings of the conflict. They shed a comprehensive yet condensed light on the political relationships of cold war politics specific to Tibet.

The work of John Kenneth Knaus, former CIA Officer, and Carole McGranahan Ph.D. Professor University of Colorado, Boulder; both shed much needed light on the Tibetan resistance. Knaus's recollection of training Tibetan men in the mountains of Colorado revealed a part of Tibet's history that to this day continues to remain a taboo subject among many Tibetans in exile. McGranahan's work specifically on Chushi Gangdrug [Gangdruk] unlocked the reasons that this portion of Tibet's history remains as she suggests, *arrested*, awaiting the appropriate time to be released.

As an independent scholar I have relied heavily on the work of others to understand what happened to Tibet over the course of its long history. My books shelves are lined with those works, as well as copious research articles, declassified government documents, and dissertations neatly filed in computer folders by topic. Most enjoyable and revealing were the candid conversations with Tibetans living in exile from parliamentarians to monks and lay people.

When I began studying the conflict twenty years ago, I wanted to discover how it was that both sides of the narrative claim the other is at fault, my thinking was that they both can't be right. Such is the nature of conflict. I've made every effort to examine material from both sides of the conflict, though finding Chinese writing on the topic that isn't brimming with rhetorical hyperbole was and still is difficult. Occasionally, a secret document slips past the firewall but that is rare. Outside reporting from human rights organizations, journalists and analysis of China's Tibetologists' work helped to fill the gaps. All this to say that I am indebted to those who through their work I have learned much and am incredibly grateful.

Directly related to writing this book, there are also many people to thank. Firstly, the many Tibetan friends and acquaintances that have fed me literally and whose friendship has fed my thirst to understand the Tibetan culture. Tashi Dolma, Tenzin Dorjee, Tenzin Palden, Tenzin Dargye, Atse, Lobsang, Lucky, Pema Metok, Wangmo, Norzom, Geleg, Lhamo, Kunchok, Thupten, Rigzen and family, words cannot express my love and gratitude for each of you.

Enlisting the generous help of several Beta Readers was incredibly helpful in the final stages of writing. I sincerely appreciate the feedback, encouragement, and viewpoints from, Sarah Westphal, Alice Russell, Margaret McDonald, Jean Bray, Pamela Kant. Thanks to Nancy Russell, for recruiting the HP book club members, and Chad Ellis for volunteering your lovely wife as a Beta Reader.

Acknowledgments

Debbie Bengsten, your enthusiastic response to an early version of the writing was the push I needed to make it to the finish line, thank you! Dan Shutt, your meticulous and thoughtful editing is much appreciated. Without your expertise I would have been lost.

Megan Sheer, thank you for the beautiful book design you created, working with you was absolutely painless and lovely.

Julie, thank you for your help as always.

Sean, Pamela, Adrian – the bright lights in my life.

RECOMMENDED READING

Brown Halper, L., Halper, S. (2014). *Tibet: An Unfinished Story.* New York: Oxford University Press.

Johnson, T. (2011). *Tragedy in Crimson: How the Dalai Lama Conquered the World and Lost the Battle with China.* New York: Nation Books.

Knaus, K. (1999). *Orphans of the Cold War: America and the Tibetan Struggle for Survival.* New York: Public Affairs.

McGranahan, C. (2010). *Arrested Histories: Tibet, the CIA, and Memories of a Forgotten War.* Durham, NC and London: Duke University Press.

Shakya, T. (1999). *The Dragon in the Land of Snows: A History of Modern Tibet Since 1947.* New York: Penguin Compass.

Talty, S. (2011). *Escape From the Land of Snows: The Young Dalai Lama's Harrowing Flight to Freedom and the Making of a Spiritual Hero.* New York: Crown Publishers.

Van Schaik, S. (2011). *Tibet: A History.* Princeton, NJ: Yale University Press.

ABOUT
THE AUTHOR

Rebecca Orton has devoted more than two decades studying Tibetan history, culture, and politics, becoming a dedicated advocate for Tibetans worldwide. Having lived in Dharamsala, India among the Tibetan exile community, she brings an intimate perspective to stories of resilience, faith, and survival.

She currently resides in the lush state of Washington near the Puget Sound.

"The world will not be destroyed by those who do evil,
but by those who watch them without doing anything."

—Albert Einstein

www.ingramcontent.com/pod-product-compliance
Lightning Source LLC
Chambersburg PA
CBHW032122090426
42743CB00007B/423